"Approximately 1.25 million people in the UK have an eating disorder"

"Around 25% of those affected by an eating disorder are male"

"Research carried out suggests that the average duration of anorexia is 8 years"

Beat

(UK eating disorder charity)

"Jesus, your wife and your kids can't help you. Only you can! Walk like it's a flat plane, <u>easy step</u> after <u>easy step</u>"

Hayden Stagg [Stephen Graham]
(Peaky Blinders: Series 6, Episode 3)

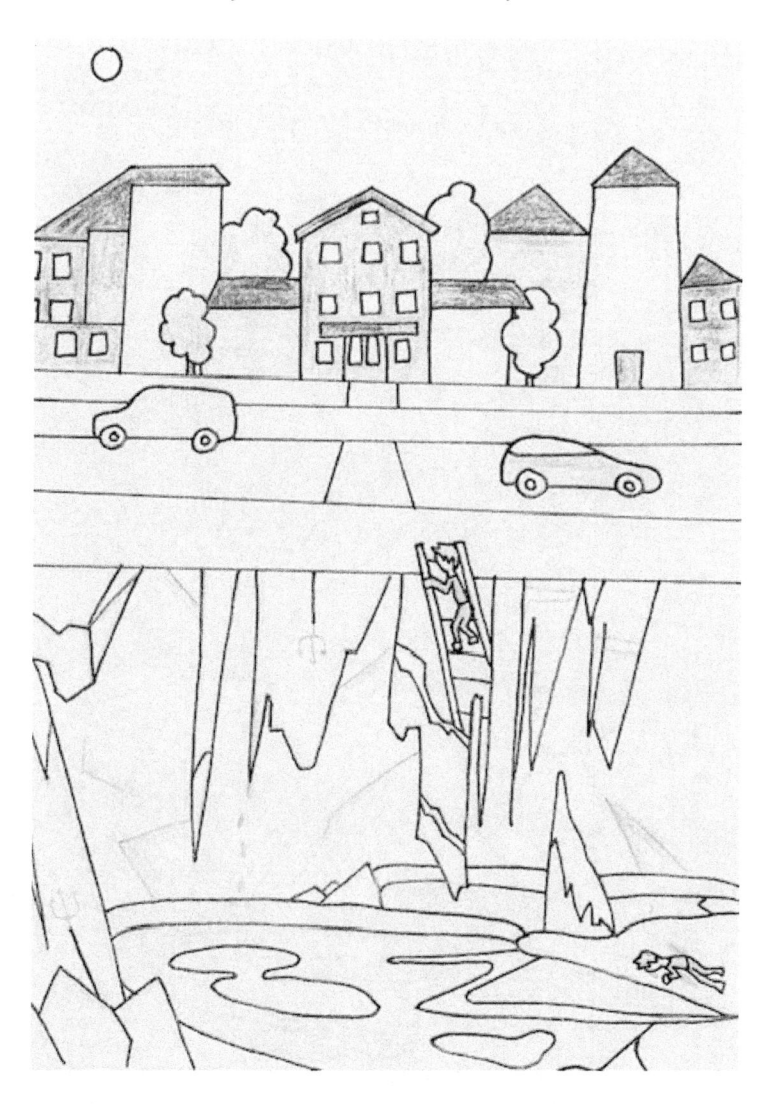

Illustrated by: *My Daughter*

PREFACE

"It's just myself, talking to myself, about myself"

Thomas Shelby
(Peaky Blinders: Series 4, Episode 6)

Hi, I'm Colin, and I genuinely work as an accountant (look it up on BBC iPlayer! ☺) ... but strictly speaking, I best identify myself as an 'AA'... an 'Anorectic Accountant'.

Welcome to my rather f*cked up world, one of decades spent living with a messy head which has seen me fall foul to numerous bouts of self-inflicting sabotage that started way back in my teens. I'm now in my 40's, happily married (I hope ☺) and father of two, but since 2014 I've led a hidden life as a fully blown professional addict... accompanied by all the rotten trimmings that go hand in hand with addiction. Over recent years I've managed to claw myself from the depths of the stinking, dark hole that goes hand in hand an **acute** case of addiction, my fingers left torn and blistered from the ascent, but to this day in both body and mind I remain an addict ... albeit one who can **just about** function in the chaos that is everyday life!

As far back as my childhood I've always yearned to connect with reading, feeling the comfort from being taken away to a far-away place of sanctuary... but I've never been able to sustain the focus nor have the mental imagery needed to sit and enjoy reading for hours on end. I was born blessed with an over-active mind, unable to concentrate for more than 5 minutes before my (sometimes multiple) thoughts wonder off in different directions. I see the letters and words on the page but find it hard to register any real meaning. I'm in total ore of people like my wife, able to immerse themselves in a good book (on the rare occasion that she actually has time), temporarily removing herself from the real world.

Writing comes with similar challenges, although it's not evident in my day-to-day life, especially to those I work with in the complex world of financial services. Whilst this book has proved to be a massive personal gamechanger for me, it's also a tough slog…typing, deleting, re-typing, deleting, and so on. Towards the end of what has been my first journey into writing, some new insight emerges into workings of my mind which has not only helped me put some long overdue missing pieces of my life jigsaw in place, it's also explained why both reading and writing have always felt alien to me… but I shan't spoil the surprise in the preface!

Authenticity is a characteristic of significant personal importance to me. When the brainwave registered that I should document a personal account of a '40's' guy in his 7-year battle (9 by the end of the book) with anorexia nervosa, I made a promise from the outset that I'd be 'real'… me, not someone I envisaged the reader would want me to be. Living through the trauma of a personal crisis at the hands of addiction has built up a huge amount of pent-up emotion and frustration in me, so I've written this book verbatim, a way of bringing my deep-rooted thoughts, and feelings to the surface. Coming from a working-class background, verbatim involves the odd expletive used here and there. In a literary sense I've taken come creative inspiration from the genius and all-round potty mouth that is Sir Billy Connolly, who once said "I know thousands of words – but I still prefer f*ck"…. hilarious!

Despite the natural desire to always stay true to myself, for too long now I've pretended to the outside world to be someone I'm not, a skill that all addicts (like me) become masters of. In truth, my mastery of performing arts, fooling the outside world into seeing me as a confident (but not overly), career focused guy, developed well before the onset of addiction. Over the years I've come to learn that this is down overwhelming fear of abandonment, borne out of childhood experiences. Put simply,

I've always wanted to be liked!

Ever since I managed to drag myself out of the deepest, darkest depths of despair, the result of an unintended relationship with anorexia, I've established a conviction to speak my mind. When you've lost years of your life conforming to the controlling voice of an inner 'addict' (which for the record is still there today) it can bring out the rebel in you. I'm by no means a loose cannon and actually see myself as a pretty balanced and constructive guy, but I'm fed up with aspects of the modern life that resist well-formed opinions, just because they might sit outside of the standard narrative we're **meant** to follow. It's perfectly okay to disagree with someone, but all too often we're now seeing the response pitched in a entirely disagreeable manner.

The content of this book is **me**...opinionated and written without the grammatical precision you'd expect from an Oxbridge educated author. But the words come from the heart, aiming to bring to life a crippling encounter with mental ill-health and addiction. It will provide you with an in-depth account of how... the f*ck... I ended up sat here, continuing to live a life wedded to an eating disorder I first developed back in 2014. I'm also using it as a means to journal my way through what I hope to be a journey back from anorexia to a fully recovered state.

My primary aim in writing this book is to connect with other 'addicts' out there, hoping to enlighten their minds to the possibility of change and with any luck, stop a few of them from following the same long and treacherous path I've walked over recent years. At the same time, I hope to appeal to the more cognitively balanced among us who simply feel frustrated with life, helping them to realise they are far from alone in their thinking.

Unlike other publications in the 'self-help' genre, this book isn't just about me. It also provides a very frank take on how the complex and arguably f*cked up nature of our modern-day world continues to drive growth in the clear and present psychological pandemic we're witnessing. Where it does crossover with other books in the same genre, is the opportunity it's given me to document a personal account of my journey to hell and back, the final destination hopefully being the point I finally gain full control over my inner demons.

If it makes it to publication and you've read this preface, deciding to place it back on the shelf, I genuinely hope you enjoy reading whatever you've exchanged your hard-earned cash for. If you've taken a step further and tapped your credit card, I hope you'll find the content thought provoking… whether you're a fellow addict, know an addict, or simply interested in reading the story of one of an increasing number of men who've battled with their mind during life.

I sincerely hope you enjoy the read!

The Fallible Man

WHO AM I?

HOW THE HELL DID I ARRIVE HERE?

CHAPTER 1
The Functioning Addict

"Addiction is a treatable, chronic medical disease involving complex interactions among brain circuits, genetics, the environment, and an individual's life experiences. People with addiction use substances or engage in behaviours that become compulsive and often continue despite harmful consequences"

American Society of Addiction Medicine

OR

"Like a soul without a mind, in a body without a heart, (I'm) missing every part"

Massive Attack, Unfinished Sympathy (1991)

A widely recognised theme that increases one's propensity to an encounter with an addiction led illness during life is a traumatic experience (in the past or present). Although at present it remains scientifically unproven, there's also a growing argument that genetic factors also play into our chances of being hooked by one or more of the catalogues of ways in which an addiction can manifest. The stark reality is that there is no golden ticket available to forewarn whether we could be drawn in by temptation at some stage or simply stroll through life unscathed. The only golden ticket I have is the stark observation that the ever-increasing level of complexity dished up by the modern world is leaving a growing number of people at risk.

Everyone knows that addiction can manifest in a multitude of different ways. The usual, but far from all-encompassing suspects sit with alcohol, illegal and prescription drugs, gambling, sex, with social media emerging as a new category over recent years. It should also be recognised that other manifestations do exist, carrying the same controlling characteristics, but they are generalised as mental health conditions (e.g., a multitude of different eating disorders and forms of self-harm). One thing everyone would benefit from recognising is that addiction and mental illness are not mutually exclusive. They go hand in hand and regardless of how an addiction manifests, the potential harm it can cause is equal in all cases.

The devastating effects that an extreme case of addiction has on the life of an addict and the family and friends surrounding them is now widely recognised, mainly due to media attention centering on high profile cases across the worlds of film, television, and music. But it's the cases we've all seen in the world of sport that stick in the forefront of my mind.

As a genuine lifelong supporter of Chelsea FC, a club I once followed as if I'd been indoctrinated into a religious cult, it's deep in my DNA to have zero sympathy for any rival London club or anyone attached... especially when it comes to Spurs and West Ham. Call it a nonsensical, immature mindset, but every deep-rooted football fan will say exactly the same about their team's local rivals. But, in my case, I'll never forget how the age old script changed when witnessing Paul Merson, a genius at the heart of the 90's Arsenal midfield, when he sat in front of the British press, a man visibly broken by an addiction to alcohol and drugs. It was 1995 and at the ripe old age of 17 with the invincible mindset that all teenagers have, I'd never considered that I too could ultimately succumb to a similar fate later in life... one that would eventually see me wedded to the crippling demands of Anorexia Nervosa. My experience at the hands of addiction would leave me physically and mentally beaten with both my marriage and career close to collapse. From what I've read, Paul Merson did manage to win the war against his drug and alcohol addiction, but he sadly went on to lose millions through gambling.

When addiction leaves its victim in a visibly rock-bottom state in life it normally sparks feelings of empathy inside anyone who carries an ounce of humanity running through their DNA. The unquestionable and hugely positive strides we've made across society over recent years to finally open up the 'Pandora's Box' that is the subject of mental health, has in some respects created a growing sense of false comfort that issues like addiction are either clearly visible to see with our own eyes, or people will simply very open about our problems. The reality is, and I can say this from where I stand today, there's a large and growing (in my opinion) population of underground addicts, invisible to the naked eye… those who for whatever reason are trapped in a vicious daily cycle of crippling addiction led behaviours, but crucially, are able to function well enough, and in some cases excel in day-to-day life, ensuring they largely go unnoticed. These members of society, which as things stand today, I remain one of, are the 'Functioning Addicts'.

What defines a 'Functioning Addict'?

It would go something like this… "someone who's daily existence is dominated in by a single or series of consistent yet health destroying (mental and/or physical) inner needs, as a means to simply provide a false sense of stability in everyday life. They know full well that their response to their mind's demands leave them in a constant state of turmoil, trapped in a vicious cycle of harmful behaviours … but they continue to conform to these demands, largely through fear of an unimaginable backlash that could manifest from within. But, despite the feeling, close enough to that living in a world of solitary confinement, a functioning addict remains able to muster the strength to skillfully operate to an extent that their underlying addiction largely goes unnoticed by others around them"

My believe is the number of people living with addiction, holding a vice like grip on there every thought and next step, yet managing to juggle the demands of home, family, and work, was already on the rise way before Covid-19 turned our world upside down. But, since arriving on UK shores in 2020, the pandemic has undoubtably served to accelerate an already growing problem, evidenced by the sharp rise in those trying access public health and charity addiction services. These services have now reached breaking point with demand outstripping supply in multiples.

Who am I?

It's only right that I'm completely honest from the start. I'm no psychologist or therapist, with absolutely zero medical training that would all me to provide qualified advice on mental health matters. I'm better described as an 'average Joe', one of the countless of guys minding his own business as they walk past you on your local high street. Born in the late 70's I grew up in a solid working-class home in northwest London with good old fashion values of grafting hard for the family, being open and honest, and priding oneself on maintaining a high level of morale integrity. I've also got a tendency to crack the odd wise crack in everyday life, and don't mind using the odd curse here and there to help make a point… in an appropriate setting of course!

While I may lack the right letters after my name that qualify me to write about the workings of the mind, I'm probably just as qualified as any medically trained practitioner. Why? Well, I've ended up taking a rather more morbid route in my studies, serving a now 8-year apprenticeship with a lived-in experience of addiction. My training, which to be frank was something I wish I'd never had, has given me a deep-rooted understanding of the mind of an addict.

I'm a pretty straight-talking guy in his 40's who has successfully won a series of tactical battles over recent years to pull myself out of the deeper depths of an addiction crisis. But as things stand today, I'm yet to deal the lethal blow to my inner enemy, which would see me finally win the war.

My Purpose

To take you into the workings of daily life in the mind of an addict, but importantly, someone who from an outsider's perspective, displays few signs of challenge, seemingly able function well in life. Alongside this, I'll provide some frank views from an 'insider' on some of the primary causes of a complex but growing modern day addiction crisis, including some of the reasons that explain why we've failed to tackle the issue. All of this with a little sarcasm, satire and honest opinion thrown in for good measure.

I won't leave anyone who reads this book feeling any more f*cked up than they did at the point they turned the cover to read the first page... I'm banking on the fact that unless you're a little morbid (nothing wrong with that), the chances are that you've bought a book about a guy struggling with addiction because either yourself or someone close to you has been touched by similar challenges in life

A sweeping generalisation, based on my reading, is that whilst books and mainstream/social media content sat in the genre of wellbeing/mental health have an underlying positive intent, there's often a theme pointing towards fixing a single, isolated area of our lifestyle, with an implied promise that change will leave you feeling on top of the world. It's unquestionable that the commercial sector has cottoned on to the fact that there's big money to be made by convincing us to change the way we lead our life as a means to protect our wellbeing, even if we don't recognise an inherent need to change. Whilst I see nothing but benefit from any attempt to raise awareness on how we address potential dangers to our wellbeing, the increasing commercialisation of the subject does leads me to question the objectivity of the messaging.... In short, I've not written this book as a means to boost my income!

This book hasn't been written as a means to sell yet another diatribe of lifestyle fixes you absolutely need to make if you're to stand any chance of arriving at that faraway place in life that is a utopian state of body and mind... usually in just four weeks! How you live your life is entirely up to you, although I sympathise if like me, you're finding yourself left increasingly frustrated with broader elements of the state system and social media that are seemingly driving guilt into the minds of those who choose not to live life in line with prescribed narrative. I'm fed up with the plethora of wealthy celebrities who hide their own human insecurities and faults behind a cyber life portrayed as perfection, constantly signalling their virtue in a bid to persuade us mere mortals how to live our lives (Gary Lineker comes top of my list). The number of boxes we now need to tick to reach a false state of online self-worth is becoming ever more ridiculous... I must go vegan to show I care for our planet, give up alcohol to prove that nights out are just as enjoyable without a beer (which they aren't!), celebrate to the world every time I hit my daily 10,000 step milestone, and of course, show how inclusive I am by illustrating my deep understanding of each and every one of the growing list of gender identities. Yes, I'm being flippant, but I've absolutely no intention of causing any offence (it's merely the humour I was born with). The point I'm trying to make is actually a serious one. The lifestyle and moral propaganda that we're increasingly being bombarded with can leave the average person who simply chooses not to or can't afford to live within the prescribed narrative, questioning their own self-worth. There's also a broader question... "what's the f*cking point in living" if you feel you can't exercise your right to freedom of choice without being looked down upon? A fulfilling life is built on the foundations of balance and the freedom to opt out without judgement.

You'll be glad to know that I'm now standing down from my soapbox...for now!

Rather selfishly, alongside the odd rant, I'm aiming to use the power of journaling to test a remarkably simple theory, most famously used in the world elite sport, in an attempt to help me finally overcome the world of addiction I still live in. If the test fails, I'll have done a shed load of typing destined for my laptop data bin, but I'm actually okay with that.

If it leads to personal success or I remain stuck where I am, I'm pretty sure the experience is going to help me gain an even deeper understanding of my own issues!

I won't promise at the outset that by the end you'll be bouncing around like Zebedee (google it if you're under 40) having been redeemed from each of your lifestyle sins. But, if having read it, it's enabled you to recognise emerging elements or already acute levels of self-harm in your life, I'm hoping it will prove to be a source of help... assuming that's what you're looking for?

And Finally

This is probably going to sound like a counter intuitive statement in a book aiming to paint a picture of the harm that addiction can cause, written by a self-confessed functioning addict…. If you live your life with repetitive, self-harming behaviours, it's not a prerequisite that you need to change anything. For example, if you're someone who chooses to drink a bottle of red every evening, you'd be pretty daft if you're not already aware of the potential health risks associated with consuming 60+ units of alcohol every week. But, if you genuinely enjoy your nightly bottle of red in full knowledge of the risks, and that bottle doesn't become a need, you crack on and glug away. You already know the dangers associated with his part of your lifestyle, but equally, you've got every right to live your life as you wish. However, if that nightly bottle is becoming or has become a hard-wired rule that you "must" to adhere to, one that strikes fear from within if circumstances challenge your ability to meet the need... speaking from personal experience, it's probably a problem you would benefit from trying to address before it gets worse.

CHAPTER 2
How the hell did I end up here?

"Early-life abuse and neglect have significant and long-lasting effects."

"Until early-life trauma is resolved, adult life relational issues are likely to manifest."

"This can take the form of addictions, trouble feeling and expressing emotions, psychological disorders, and more."

Psychology Today

How did I, an all-round sensible guy with so much to be thankful for in life, end up following a path to the point of self-destruction?... one hell of a bombshell question to ask yourself, but one I suspect is becoming ever more common in today's world.

I had a great job in the City of London and despite the absence of university education, I was earning a 'good wedge', on a par with my Oxbridge educated work colleagues. I had brilliant family life, loving marriage, two healthy kids, great mum and stepfather, a nice annual holiday to look forward to, and a great family home in West Sussex with a perfectly manageable mortgage. I never knew the 'Englishman's castle' I'd worked so hard to build could be invaded and infiltrated by a dark enemy force.

My mental health car crash, that hit me in the November of 2014, had in fact been a slow burn until that point. But just like some of motorway collisions we hear about in the news, the impact was instantaneous and brutal. In truth, my cognitive health had spiraling downwards from as far back as my early teenage years, like a saucepan of milk on the hob, simmering gently to start with, but if you take your eye of it, it'll gradually start to rise, and with no warning you find yourself cleaning up one big f*cking mess! And what a mess it created, with those closest to me left completely blind and incapable of dealing with what proved to be a highly complex clean-up operation.

All too often, whilst a traumatic event can trigger a mental health crisis, the underlying cause lies in the past, leaving someone unknowingly on the brink of a crisis situation for years. The traumatic event that ultimately pulled the trigger in my life, occurred at the age of 36, having witnessed my father's very slow and agonising death. I'd been edging slowly towards the cliff edge of sanity for years, but it was witnessing first-hand how cruel life could be that finally pushed me over the edge, sending me and my immediate family crashing down to the rocks beneath.

My dad was one of those guys that in many ways others around him probably aspired to be like. To the outside world, back in his 40's, my dad had everything. He was a sales director for a leading global tech business and travelled the world with work, earning big money that funded a comfortable upper-middle class lifestyle many would dream of … big house, a new car every couple of years, luxurious holidays, horse riding lessons for the kids… and all the other trimmings you can think of. He was also always the life and sole of the social scene in every drinking hole he frequented… a classic case of having the 'gift of the gab', always full of banter and able to build new friendships at the drop of a hat.

The life of 'everything' my dad led was somewhat different to the one I grew up in. He and my mum separated when I was 8, as he left to start a new life with his second wife, which produced my two half-sisters, both of whom I've retained a strong bond with to this day.

Despite the first 8 years of my life spent with mum and dad, I honestly can't recall there ever being family unit. I can count on one hand the times I remember the three of us being together as a family, limited to a family holiday in Portugal when I was 6, maybe 7, and one Christmas when mum and dad hosted a party for their friends who used to drink with my dad down the local social club. The only memory I have of just dad and I being together before he and mum separated was the morning of my 5th birthday when he presented me with a brand-new BMX, watching me practice on my new wheels down the alleyway at the back of our house before school... the memory still makes me smile to this day!

It's fair to say that when I was growing up in the 1980's family life was different to the way it is now, with circumstances very much 'of their time' ... men in the pub, women and children at home, cooking dinner and causing mischief respectively. My dad was always a drinker, but in his mid 40's alcohol became a more visible and concerning problem in his life. The same script as the one that played out in my paternal grandfather's life was being re-written, except this time, earlier in life. The addiction switch in his brain had been turned on, leaving him at the mercy of fully blown alcoholism... not that at any point did ever entertain the concept that he may have had a problem.

Looking back now, Dad's downfall from grace which started in his mid 40's and ending the day he died aged 62 was both sad and beyond all belief. Over this period of his life, he had two further failed marriages, drinking to excess saw his career flushed down the pan, and he lost more or less everything he owned. In the last couple of years of life he'd ended up living in bedsit provided by the local council, spending what seemed like every waking hour drinking and smoking. Over that period, I can't recall a single time when I spoke to him when he was actually sober.

Living in poverty is a humbling sight for anyone with just a single ounce of empathy, but when it's seemingly self-inflicted, it can be an incredibly frustrating thing to witness. To any outsider, all the evidence at the time suggested he'd simply chosen to pi** his life up the wall. But as time has gone by, I've slowly come to the view that wasn't actually the case... he was a deeply flawed person with many positive attributes, but ill and however frustrating it was for my sisters and I, too stubborn and proud to recognise it.

Graphic reference to end-of-life experiences can be triggering for some. If you fall into this category, feel free to excuse yourself from reading the following handful of paragraphs... I've inserted page markers at the start and end so you know when you can start reading again

◆◆◆

"If you can be with a loved one when they die, you should. Her hands getting cold as the circulation shuts down, her breathing getting heavy, the death rattle. Bearing witness to a death is an incredibly intimate thing. You should be there, not because it's easy – it isn't – but because one day you'll want someone to hold your hand."

Jimmy Carr
(Before & Laughter)

The quote above, taken from a brilliant book written by Jimmy Carr, was his own reflections having been there when his mum died. I absolutely loved reading 'Before and Laughter' but my only experience witnessing death has left me with a very different perception.

Late in 2013 my dad sat my two (half) sisters and I down and explained that he'd been diagnosed with cancer of the esophagus. The "big C" always sparks feelings of dread, but this form of cancer that gets little airtime is notorious for having one of the lowest survival rates.

From that day, it took a mere seven months to receive the call from one of my sisters, letting me know he'd been rushed into hopital after he was found collapsed in his flat, excrement everywhere and in an all-round appalling state of health. The prognosis didn't look good, but he did muster enough strength after a few days to be transferred to a hospice in Farnborough, Hampshire. This followed a short visit to his flat to collect some essential belongings. I can still see that skeleton of a once fit man, using all of his remaining strength just to walk the few yards from the building entrance to the ambulance waiting to transport him to the hospice, me holding his belongings, him stubbornly refusing any help getting to the vehicle.

The hospice was a real place of sanctuary where wholly underpaid carers treated him with the upmost respect and dignity during the final weeks of his life. During dad's stay, I'd spent days there keeping him company and helping him all those things we all take for granted in daily life like getting to a lavatory and having a wet shave. This went on for weeks, me crashing at my sister's house.

With all this going on in my life, the pressure that came with my job working for a global insurer in city never eased. Whilst there was a degree of muted sympathy for my situation, the reality is that business doesn't just stop because someone is dying. This meant I ended up spending days on end in the hospice trading emails, dialing into conference calls, doing my best to lead a large team, all while a mere stone's throw away, my dad was slowly eaten up by cancer.

During the last couple of weeks of my dad's life I pretty much lived at the hospice, sleeping in a bedroom they reserved for family of patients facing an imminent outcome to their illness. By day I sat watching his face and torso slowly become more and more emaciated, his legs ballooned by retained water as his internal organs slowly shutdown. As a poor and ill-advised means of distraction, I kept working, even to the point he slowly lost consciousness. It took until his final day of life for me to finally stop working. From that point, alongside wonderful and genuinely caring nurse, I sat watching the life drain from body, minute by minute, then second by second.

All too often death is a slow and painful process for its victim, but also for anyone witnessing it. Whilst we're led to believe it happens quickly, just as Hollywood portrays, the reality is often very different. For their own sake, I have vowed to do my best to convince my kids to stay away when I reach the same stage in life. I want them to remember me as I their dad now rather than what I became during the final days of life.

♦♦♦

If you decided to skip the last section, you're now safe to continue reading....

Naturally I was devastated that my dad, far from an old man, had to go through the pain and suffering that cancer dealt him, but with absolutely no intent to speak ill of the dead, it feels contextually important to say that my old man was never genuinely there for me as a father, most notably when I was growing up. I've no doubt he would have bailed me out in a crisis, but a mix of his own childhood learnings from what sounded like a distant approach to fatherhood that my grandad took and him moving on to prioritise his new family, meant our relationship was always somewhat transactional... akin to one you'd have with a friend at colleague.

As a child I used to see dad every fortnight, the excitement always building as the Saturday morning pick-up approached. Despite his decision to leave mum and I, I idolised him.... flash cars, designer clothes and ever popular with his friends. But looking back now, the limited time we did spent together was largely structured around what he wanted to do, rather than things that would build a genuine and long-lasting bond with his son. He'd usually pick me up, then drop me off at my nans for a few hours, whilst he and my grandad went to the social club for a solid lunchtime session. Thankfully for me, if angels exist on earth, my nan was one of them. In my childhood years through to my teens, nan was like my second loving parent.

The one saving grace in the relationship between dad and I was when Chelsea were playing at home. Despite Chelsea's status in the 80's, lightyears behind where the club stands today, my support for the club had parallels with being indoctrinated into a religious cult. As a kid I lived and breathed Chelsea FC, but looking back on it now, I think this was merely a subconscious effort in a bid to seek the recognition I desired from my equally obsessed Dad.

It took me a few years after dad's passing to finally realise that so much of my path in life until well into my 30's, had been a product of an ongoing childlike fear of abandonment.... like a subconscious way of always trying to be recognised in an effort to establish an ounce of self-worth. I'd achieved top end GCSE and A-Level grades, landed a professional qualification, and secured regular promotions to Director level, lived in a nice house, fathered two healthy kids and was in a stable marriage… With exception of my marriage and family, that childlike need to prove a sense of self-worth created most of these things. At the same time, it also led me down the path of crippling levels of anxiety, all centered on an intense fear of failure.

What eventually became an obsession with achieving perfection, fueled by a fear of failure, started when I in secondary school. I was always a conscientious student, but it was the year leading up to my GCSEs when I first presented self-harming behaviours. From an academic perspective, I'd pitch myself as just above average, with a hard work ethic lifting me up another notch. But months before I was due to sit my GCSE exams, I found myself revising up to 50 hours a week in addition to my time spent at school. I'd become fixated with getting top grades. As my school friends all had health social lives, I was spending every minute of my free time studying, becoming a complete recluse and with the exams approaching in the summer of 1994, the overwhelming pressure I'd placed on myself took me near to meltdown.

Despite the months of self-imposed hard labor, running the risk of exhaustion leading to exam failure, I achieved good grades. The benefit of hindsight tells me this was probably the worst outcome, as it served to hard wire the false connection between self-punishment and success into my daily thinking.

Moving on to my A-Levels, the step up in difficulty meant one thing... to push myself even harder! By May 1997, just before sitting my A-Level exams, I'd pretty much reached the point of self-destruction, regularly breaking down at home under the sheer weight of personal pressure. But yet again, I did well, achieving a clean sweep of A grades.

Despite the self-induced trauma I'd just put myself through, all to avoid the potential but unknown risk of a disappointed father, I then made a seemingly insane decision go to university (studying Politics and Social Policy at Brunel). I'd already pushed myself to the limit with a daily 10-12 hours study regime (on top of classes), that went on for the duration of the final year leading up to my A-Levels. There was simply no more time in the day I could find to cope with the inevitable step up to a degree. I spend 3 months as the only 'fresher' who may as well have set up their halls of residence in the university library, whilst everyone else was enjoying the freedom from parental control. Mentally broken, it was the first time in my life that I gave up. My dad didn't really say much, but I got the distinct impression that missing up the chance to be the first member of the family to secure a degree did leave him disappointed.

Having managed to pick myself up after my brief stint at university, I headed straight to work, opting for an apprenticeship route to build a career in finance. I knew that a 'profession' would look good in my dad's eye, given how successful he'd been at work. I ended up studying for my accountancy exams whilst working full time, one of the toughest career paths to take. At the time when I made the decision I'd clearly forgotten my past experiences in education, making it a seemingly ridiculous choice to make. By then, my now wife and I were living together, which gave her full sight of the torture I'd put myself (and her) through, just to achieve exam success. But I did it, three long years later, I landed my qualification as a Chartered Accountant. Still lacking any degree of content with life after qualifying, the obsession then moved on to flogging myself at work in search of promotion after promotion. This took me well into my 30's, by then, earning a salary well into six figures, but deeply unhappy and physically shattered from two decades of emotional self-harm.

By my mid 30's, stressed, tired and hating my professional life, my obsession with achieving perfection was so extreme that even the smallest human error on my part, either at work or home resulted in the self-destruction button being slammed down...." You're a f*cking worthless piece of sh*t! How the hell has your total stupidity gone unnoticed at work for so long? Your wife must be blind or plain stupid to see anything in you". Simply put, years of self-inflicted punishment had shattered any ounce of self-esteem I'd once had, leaving me with no cognitive option but to impose a barrage of self-critique.

My mum has also suffered at the hands of mental ill-health/fragility throughout her life, most notably her acute experience when I was a baby that saw her no more than a whisker away from being sectioned. To this day, she'd openly admit to being in a consistent state of varying levels of anxiety, often with little rationale to explain why. Whether it's pure coincidence, a hereditary pattern, or exposure to instability as a child, it's a funny (not in the literal sense) that whilst the path may have been different, I ended up taking a similar journey through life to the one my mum took.

Despite the challenges she encountered, my mum and my stepfather, who joined her, and I when I was 11, have been nothing but brilliant parents to me. Growing up, my homelife was supportive with plenty of love and solid role modelling. We never had much money, my mum working as a bank clerk and my stepdad a butcher, but I had what I'd describe as a solid working-class upbringing, assisted by my ever-supportive paternal nan. Yes, there were troubled parts of my childhood, but the solid adult roles models present, helped me develop the guiding core values I still live by to this day… honesty, integrity, respect for others, kindness and trustworthiness.

Not long after my father had been laid to rest, an inner anger started to emerge and rapidly gained strength. Both mind and body felt like a pressure cooker waiting to explode. I became increasingly irritable, not just with myself, but others around me. I'd even go as far as saying I'd become nasty, taking my anger out on loved ones, largely in the direction of my wife. It never got physical, but if I hadn't have decided to leave home for a period at the back end of 2014, going to stay with my mum, who knows what could have happened. The thought of how it could have played out still scares me to this day.

It took years of soul searching to finally understand the root cause of why I'd become the man I was. Back in 2014 I'd naturally linked the overnight transformation in my personality with the trauma I'd experienced watching my father die so slowly and painfully. With help from therapy, the realisation eventually came that witnessing my father's passing was merely the trigger.

The underlying cause of my switch from a respectable family man to a volatile and highly unpredictable person was down to the personal sacrifice I'd made by just being there for father, right up to the point he took his last breath. It was the human thing to do, being there for someone suffering so badly, but those final weeks tore a piece of my sole away. That genuine care, love and support I gave during that period had never been reciprocated by my dad during my childhood, when all I ever wanted was a close father/son relationship. I was left deeply angry with myself, for allowing to be exposed to such a vulnerable situation, for not being assertive, for not keeping my distance as my dad had done with me over the years. But I couldn't stand back and allow him to die alone. Ultimately, displaying such compassion had led me down the path of self-hate and ultimately self-destruction. I'd found my new best friend, anorexia nervosa.

Since 2014, the battle to reach a point of stability proved to be an arduous journey, but I finally managed to reach a "functioning" state in 2019. Since then, I've been left in a state of limbo, fearing the transition from functioning to living… however ridiculous that sounds! Therapy has given me the strength to grow empathy for my father. He too was an addict, with a hard adult exterior hiding the pain of an inner child, using alcohol as his way of coping, keeping the pain firmly locked away inside. The natural 'go to' reason to explain a why a mental health crisis has been triggered, is a traumatic event. In a world addicted (excuse the pun) to quick fixes, it's the easy answer…. But in many cases, the underlying reason sits far deeper within than we first realise.

CHAPTER 3
Life as a 'Functioning Addict'
(Trust me... it's pretty damn f*cked up!)

I've thought long and hard to find a way to summarise what it feels like during the transitionary period from living with full blown anorexia nervosa to the point where the underlying illness remains present but you're able to function in life. I'm conscious that it's probably going to sound over dramatic but the only way I can attempt to bring justice to the scale of the challenge is to draw a parallel with my own perception of what it must have been like to have fought in the battle of Stalingrad. This battle proved to be one of hardest fought and bloodiest battles of WW2 that left the Russian city of Stalingrad in utter ruins and took a reported casualty toll in excess of 2 million. Fought in the depths of the city, literally street by street, it was one of the toughest of WW2 and left left Joseph Stalin's namesake city and the attacking German military units flattened. It's widely regarded by most historians as the point when the tide of the war finally turned in favour of the allied forces. The enemy, the German forces, and in my case the eating disorder that still resides within me, had been severely wounded, pushed into retreat, but was still yet to surrender.

Winning the battle to restore one's physical health to a stable, functioning state often takes casualties along the way, primarily the strain the journey can have on close relationships which can easily become severed beyond all repair. This alongside the mental trauma every anorectic endures during the fight usually leaves lifelong scares. Whilst victory may have been declared in an arduous battle to reach stability, the war inside the mind continues, with the fight moved from standard military tactics to guerrilla warfare.

After 5 years feeling like I was one of those front-line Russian soldiers fighting through the streets of Stalingrad, capturing yards of territory, only to be pushed back a little and then retake the precious yards lost, I finally reached a stable state of physical health in 2019. I've remained there until this day, now 3 years on.

I'm now able to function in life. I hold down an incredibly demanding job, work long hours and do my best to be a "21st century man", doing my best to contribute to the family home alongside my teammate (my wife) covering school runs, after-school clubs, cooking and household chores. I even manage to carve out time to work alongside two other coaches running a football team in my now hometown of East Grinstead that my son plays for. F*ck knows where I've found any time to write this book!

Despite my outwardly visible ability to manage the demands of day-to-day life, the reality is that simply getting through each day remains a constant battle for me, a battle against self-inflicted mental exhaustion, driven by the need to adhere to a series of strict and punishing self-imposed rules. If I break one of the rules all hell breaks loose, leading to an inevitable internal backlash. To illustrate, try to visualise a scenario where you're confronted by the most intimidating person your imagination can create… someone snarling like a rabid pit bull, in your face hurling vile abuse, the situation telling you that a physical attack is imminent. In this scenario do you defend yourself with an assertive stance by standing up to them with words of reason, or pre-empt the attack by landing the first blow, this move carrying the risk of unknown consequences? Or do simply back down, curling up into a fetal position, giving the aggressor a powerful sense of victory without any need for physical violence. The bully you're visualising lives inside the mind of thousands likeminded anorectics, carrying an overbearing command over them, be they in a state of serious malnutrition, or in a state functioning health as I am today.

The inner voice becomes overwhelmingly powerful when

anorexia nervosa leaves someone dangerously underweight, carrying a shrunken brain mass with little to no cognitive strength to even conceptualise being able to think rationally. This leaves the anorectic caught up in a viscous cycle of ever reducing weight, with the brain becoming less and less capable of defending the body against the 'voice' with each passing day. Unlike some debilitating physical illnesses, treatable with medication or surgery, the only way to navigate out of an eating disorder led addiction crisis is through the application of sheer cognitive strength. If someone is unlucky enough to enter the danger zone as I once did, carrying a brain mass estimated at less than half it's normal size (according to my specialist), it goes some way to explain why some victims never manage to muster the strength to fight the compulsive thoughts and associated actions the disease feeds on. It's an incredibly disturbing fact that anorexia nervosa carries the highest death rate attributable to any mental health condition. I count myself as one of the lucky ones. If it hadn't had been for the love and support from my wife, mother, stepfather, and best friend Richard, who collectively gave me strength to claw my way back to a functioning state, I'm not sure whether I'd be here today.

On the whole I'd say I'm perceived by most to be an everyday guy... albeit still a little on the skinny side! Outwardly, to those who don't know me well, I suspect I come across as confident, assertive, and someone never afraid to voice a structured opinion if I feel strongly about something. But the truth is, it's all one big f*cking front. The reality is that whilst I've always lacked confidence, the crumbs of any genuine belief I once had in myself have been swept away over the years living my life adhering to a strict set of daily rules, all centered on the theme of "I must". These "musts" are an all-too-common part of an anorectic's life, illustrating the OCD traits that go hand in hand with the condition. Living life with this condition necessitates having to adhere to multiple "musts" that are often structured in a neat hierarchy. I refer to this hierarchy as primary and secondary "musts".

To my knowledge, in almost all cases of anorexia nervosa the primary "musts", being the most powerful compulsions, normally present as "I must hit my daily exercise target" and "I must not exceed my already low daily calorific allowance / reduce it even more". How much exercise I "must" do or how little I "must" eat varies from one case to another, the common theme being that as the illness takes it's hold, these self-imposed targets only ever go one way…. they become harder and evermore more physically and emotionally destructive.

The anorexic voice places constant demands on its 'host' to continually exceed the targets set. Whether it's just one less calorie or one more step in a day, it rewards its host with an enormous sense of self-gratifying endorphins when targets are beaten, delivering a feeling similar to that experienced when an athlete sets a new PB (personal best). Just like an athlete's reaction, once a new PB is in place the target bar is raised with energy now focused on beating it again. With every new PB comes a more punishing target that "must" be smashed the next day, a cycle that can easily continue until someone is hospitalised or in extreme cases, loses the fight to live.

I classify myself as an addict but the mechanics and rationale that underpins the addict mindset still remains one big f*cking mystery to me. How can the mind develop to form two distinctly different voices from within?... the rational voice and the addict voice… both in a constant state of conflict, with the latter being the dominant force. I wake up each morning with the addict voice whispering away, initially leading me into a false sense of security with promises of change… "I'll only swim one kilometre today (40 lengths)", "Sod cooking tonight, we'll grab fish and chips". By 11am, the voice is now loud, with its sentiment having swung 180 degrees … "You will swim two kilometres and f*ck the takeaway, it's a skinless chicken breast and salad for you tonight!". Same f*cking scenario every day!!!

The mystery associated with the mind of an addict goes some way to explain why there are so many instances of relapse with addiction. I've now got myself to a state whereby I'm able to function in daily life, but I'm constantly looking over my shoulder with a sense of fear that I could once again become the person I once was.

"Most rules are self-imposed; it's you holding onto an old idea. Your preconceptions about how things 'should' be are what stop you from becoming a different person."

Jimmy Carr
(Before & Laughter)

Another brilliant quote from Carr's book that I felt compelled to use given its masterful simplicity in bringing to life just why so many addicts stay wedded to a life of addiction. "Preconceptions" form what feels like an overwhelmingly difficult barrier to change. To provide a sense, let me illustrate by taking you inside the mechanics of my mind... that guarantee with each and every sunrise I wake up to the same f*cking Groundhog Day!

The Primary "Musts"

"I must hit my exercise target"

Pre anorexia, I got heavily into long distance running. I spent 7 years loving the sport, completing countless 10k's, well over 30 half marathons and 6 full marathons, my personal best over the 26.2 miles a little over 3hrs. I even went as far as setting up a 10k race in my town of residence. With the inaugural race taking place in 2010, the East Grinstead 10k was set up in memory of Andy Ripely, who once played rugby union for England but sadly died aged 62 from prostate cancer. The annual event which continues to this day raised well over £20,000 for good causes during the 8 years I was involved. My social life revolved around running, with the long group runs on Sunday mornings becoming my Saturday night in the pub with mates. The sport also gave me a safe haven and stimulus to work through the pressures of professional life. Little did I know in the good days that it would also play a critical part in setting me on a path to a future battle with addiction.

By the time the anorectic voice had cemented itself firmly in core of my mind, it was driving me to run over 100 miles a week, getting up as early as 4:30am on weekdays to run up to 14 miles before jumping onto a train into London financial district to work a 10-12 hour day in a highly pressurised job. I'd be back home around 8pm, ram dinner down my neck, answer a few more work emails, then lights out by 10:30 for 6 hours kip before the next day's early morning chimes. No time for my kids, my wife or myself. In my darkest day's I was running/walking around 20 miles a day on a calorie intake a little over 1500.

Whilst I've made huge strides forward since the dark days, the grip of my most powerful "must", the need to exercise, remains tight. Even now, a typical weekday day for me would leave most feeling exhausted, from just the thought of it:

Morning: 30mins exercise - Walking my son to school having driven and parked the car in a spot equidistant from both my kid's schools. I then a walk my son to his school, then walk back to the car. How many other parents can you think of that manage school runs in this way? I know, it's f*cking madness, but the reality of living life with addiction is that any sense of normality is thrown out of the window.

Lunchtime: Up to 80 lengths in my local pool or a decent walk with my best pal, Cooper (the dog).

Evening: 45mins exercise – Swim or dog walk, depending on what I've done at lunchtime.

On Wednesday evenings I join the other coaches to manage midweek training for my son's football team, providing yet another opportunity to exercise. Yep, that's right (if you've clocked it) …. although I genuinely love the fact I've got an opportunity to be part of the personal and sporting development of a great group of young lads, my primary goal when it comes to training is to reward my addiction. 2-3 hours of exercise each day on top of a 10-12 hours working, and then there's the family and home related stuff to manage. It's no wonder I constantly feel f*cked which begs the obvious question… "why the hell do it?".

For people like me who clearly have strong addictive traits, exercise can easily become a double-edged sword. Everyone knows that physical activity releases endorphins into the body, an entirely natural painkiller providing an uplifting sense of euphoria. But there is an increasing amount of evidence that endorphins carry similar properties to opiates, delivering a cognitive high that can drive an unhealthy need for a greater fix next time. This situation is more common for those involved in endurance sports like long distance running. Mix my pre anorexia love of distance running with an addictive personality and a mental health crisis, I was effectively staring straight into a perfect storm, tapping into an endless supply of a free, yet perfectly legal painkilling drug to stem the flow of inner pain.

"I must not exceed my daily calorific intake allowance"

During my darkest days, like everyone else unfortunate enough to be touched by anorexia nervosa, every day was consumed by an obsession with counting calories and weighing myself multiple times. At the peak of my illness, I'd check my weight 5, maybe 6 times a day, stripping down to my underwear in what became a sole destroying effort to feel comfort in seeing my weight drop. My obsession with counting calories all consuming. I became an expert on the calorific value of every item sold in my local Sainsburys, with a weekly shop that should have taken half an hour, sometimes taking me three times as long, as I read and memorised the nutritional value of food and drink placed in the trolley. I thought about calories all day and regularly found myself counting them in my sleep at night, which was my body's biological response to its need for re-feeding.

A calorie-controlled diet remains incredibly important part of daily life for me, but I'm no longer obsessed with maintaining a running total of the calorific value of everything that enters my mouth during the course of the day. The obsession with calorie counting dissipated, but the truth is, this is only because I remain heavily constrained by the need to avoid foods my eating disorder deems unacceptable…. i.e., anything carrying a moderately high calorific value!

Whilst you'd naturally expect and be correct in assuming that the likes of McDonalds, KFC, or Indian takeaways to be on the banned list, for some reason I still fear (literally becoming frozen solid) perfectly acceptable, nutritionally balanced foods. What adds further complexity to the madness is that I'm feel compelled to abide by the most non-sensical rules that allow foods in some settings but ban them in others. Providing a full catalogue of the weird sh*t that goes on in my head every day about what I can and can't eat, in pre-determined combinations, would make pretty long and boring reading, so I'll avoid you the pain by keeping to just a few examples:

Eggs: Boiled okay, but scrambled and fried are no nos.

Cow's milk: Okay in my morning coffee but not on cereal, even skimmed… has to be a coconut or almond milk (both unsweetened).

Cheese: completely banned unless a light sprinkling in a sarnie, compensated of course by having no olive spread on the bread.

Potatoes: Jackets and boiled okay, all other variations are banned… unless it's a Saturday night which opens the door to a small handful of chips.

The whole thing is a f*cking joke, but what makes it even more ridiculous is that I'm not blind to the madness of it all. Despite this I remain constrained by the fear of the repercussions that challenging the status quo could bring.

The thing that makes the whole situation even more insane is that like so many other functioning addicts, I'm perfectly capable of holding a rational state of mind when I face the day-to-day challenges that life throws at all of us… that's what helps the functioning addict blend into society without detection. I wouldn't be able to hold down the demanding job I have involving extended working hours managing a multitude of complex and often competing demands if I couldn't make sensible judgement calls. But when it comes down to the food I consume, needed to keep my body and mind 'ship shape' to manage the demands of life, the anorectic voice puts a knife to my throat, even if I'm presented with foods that are nutritionally beneficial.

The Secondary "Musts"

It's not uncommon for anorectics like me to have a subset of rules that sit beneath the primary "musts", forming a hierarchy of primary and secondary rules. This creates a whole new level of complexity for someone to manage through, just to be seen to function normally without people from outside your trusted circle noticing strange behaviours. The interrelationships formed between rules at both primary and secondary levels create the added complexity… context to follow once I've given a flavour of my secondary rules:

"I must not eat before allotted mealtimes"

If you're thinking "WTF", this is pretty common "must" in the life of someone addicted to the false sense control that starvation provides. Even with dark days now long behind me, if I'm forced into a situation where I need to eat breakfast before 10:30, lunch before 15:00 or dinner before 21:00, my brain literally feels like it's going to explode from the resulting anxiety... similar to the implosion when the bullet hits the centre of a watermelon practice target. This won't be the first shockingly bad metaphor you'll encounter in this book.... my lacking creativity when it comes to words is either a symptom of my dyslexia or simply justification for the career I chose working with numbers (I'm guessing it's the latter).

A few weeks back I had the opportunity to join the UK CEO and senior leadership team of the company a spot of lunch. Presenting a great networking opportunity for someone who's always strived to hit the next level on the career ladder, you'd think I'd be relishing the 'networking' opportunity. But when the invite dropped into my inbox for a 13:30 lunch, Mount f*cking Vesuvius duly erupted! "OMG, 90mins before I'm allowed to eat lunch... definitely a smaller breakfast! What about my lunchtime exercise? What will the food be? Takeaway Dominos?" ... as if the CEO is going to be lay on greasy pizzas and molded chicken bites!... "Definitely a longer dog walk or swim tonight, maybe both, to compensate" ... "and something very 'healthy' for dinner, no earlier than 21:00". This is no different to the kind of mind-numbing sh*t I deal with day in, day out when the rules are threatened!

Thankfully, my lunch with the CEO and Exec team went okay. I managed (I think) to hold down a decent conversation at the table without outwardly showing the heightened anxiety running through my entire body. This was drastically helped by a spread of healthy food; salmon (no skin), loads of salad with feta cheese (I worked around the cheese), and desserts consisting of fresh fruit, cheesecake, and a rather luxurious looking chocolate tarte…. You can guessed right; I went for the sodding fruit!

If you're reading this and you're lucky enough not to have ever encountered the challenges of an eating disorder, I'm sympathetic to the view that the scenario I've just relayed is one of complete and utter madness. For those who've encountered anorexia nervosa and or other eating disorders, the reality is that this is everyday life.

"I must have a beer and a glass of red wine each evening"

The rationale side of my mind would read the following to the statement above… "good on you, you bloody well deserve a daily vice given how hard you work". But it's become such a habit, that in many ways I struggle to cope if I faced with the prospect of an evening when I don't have precisely one beer and a glass of wine. And to make a frankly daft situation even more f*cking stupid is the connecting interrelationship between this "must at the time I eat …the beer can't be consumed before 20:45 (before dinner) and the glass of wine must wait until 21:30 at the earliest (after dinner).

I'm going to struggle to turn up at work and speak to my colleagues having shared the utter insanity of my day-to-day life over the last few paragraphs… but the endgame to expose the hell that comes with an addiction led illness is far more important than reputation… so I'll just crack on.

I'd be kidding myself if I failed to recognise that an eating disorder plus the crippling episodes of OCD I experienced from my mid-teens to my late twenties probably mean I'm probably in a higher risk group when it comes to the chances of me developing an alcohol dependency. But, in my case an addiction to alcohol is an extremely low risk. I saw alcohol literally destroy the lives of both my father and grandfather, with events along their journeys taking innocent emotional casualties with them (especially my angel of a Nan who bore witness to everything). I witnessed them both die well before their time should have been up, and in my father's case, losing the status and simple human dignity he worked incredibly hard to build over his working life.

Given the high calorific and low nutritional value in alcohol, even a half a pint of beer sounds like a bloody daft thing to consume when I become physically incapacitated if faced with the prospect of eating a f*cking egg (feel free to smirk). But alcohol consumption and anorexia nervosa have more in common that you'd naturally think. In recent years sections of the medical profession have given increasing airtime to a condition known as 'Drunkorexia', a subset of the overarching eating disorder. This condition carries the normal constraints associated with anorexia nervosa, being extreme levels of control over nutritional intake and excessive exercise but includes permission to consume alcohol. This is usually a desperate attempt on the part of the addict to try and dull the inner anorectic voice. A 'drunkorectic' will still live within the daily confinement of a pre-determined calorie allowance but will swap some calories carrying nutritional value for alcohol, which has we know has no nutritional value. The associated issues unfold when the target calorie allowance is reducing, meaning the proportion of alcoholic calories increase as 'savings' normally come from sources of nutrition.

Am I an anorectic or a drunkorectic? Who knows, and frankly, who gives a t*ss? All I know is that I'll never get drunk on a single beer and glass of wine. But if I don't adhere to the "must", I still feel like I've lost control.

The 'Perfect Storm'

Appreciating that the parts of my daily life I've relayed will be difficult for any normal level-headed person to comprehend, I'll now attempt to bring the madness to life. An example of a 'perfect storm' scenario for me would be an all-day work event including an overnight stay in a nice hotel! I suspect this will sound alright for others who, like me, spend countless hours moving from one virtual Teams meeting to another on a weekday... a day out of the house, which has become a confusing place since the pandemic...the base for work, school for a period and then of course, 'normal family life. Providing a chance to get out of the house and have some free grub, a good night's sleep in a nice hotel room, and have a few drinks, all at the expense of the company, sounds great! Doesn't it? In my case, I fail to see any of the positives, and would be freaking out from the moment I receive the invite until the day arrives, knowing the scenario breaks every rule in the book. The following is something along the lines of the way my thoughts would play out:

"How the hell am I going to get a morning walk in and hit the pool later on? Maybe the hotel has a pool?... note to self... check in advance!... I could excuse myself for part of the day, citing illness, or just sneak off for a swim... no one will notice! And how the hell can I walk the dog when he's 100 miles away?... maybe move the illness excuse to the end of the day?... he won't mind waiting until 9pm for his walk". Note to reader... the walk wouldn't actually be to satisfy the dog!

"Set menus for both lunch and dinner, with no option to cater for my complex needs... could I have a plain jacket potato, no butter, instead of dauphinoise? Have you got any coconut milk for my coffee? I prefer the taste to cow's milk (not!). Any chance I can swap the beef for skinless chicken breast?... I don't like red meat". Note to reader... that's a f*cking lie!

"Drinks are likely to be flowing freely in the evening from around 7pm" ... pre-dinner 'networking', a setting I've never enjoyed... watching the career hungry brown nosing the 'big wigs' with false laughter and the risk that one slip of the working class tongue sends my own chances of a future promotion flushing down the pan. "7pm is precisely 75mins too early for me to have a drink! Got it, I'll head down and order a slimline tonic, ice and a slice… if anyone asks, it's large G&T."

"Breakfast the following morning will be way before 10:30am… I'll skip breakfast, citing the need to attend a fake conference call, wait until 10:30 and hit the cereal bar I'll pack in my bag… note two to self… pack one!... Lunch, "f*ck, it's at midday! Make your excuses, hide in the toilet, turn up towards the end and grab some fruit"

Blah, blah, f*cking blah!

I've intentionally used sarcasm in describing by reaction to a 'perfect storm' scenario. It's the only means to illustrate the utter insanity that unpins the illness that continues to walk alongside me. The fact is, it doesn't matter how an addiction may manifest, the pattern of thinking is normally the same, forcing seemingly level-headed individuals to think and behave in irrational ways, all in a vain attempt to provide a sense of safety against what they know is an entirely non-existent threat. My application of humour is a tool I've learned to use as go-to way of adding a degree of sanity back into my life, but the reality of the daily challenge faced by functioning addicts can be sole destroying!

If you're lucky enough to have never suffered with or been closely connected to someone living with addiction, don't worry if this chapter left you feeling utterly confused. Even if you've had a secondary encounter with addiction, possibly seeing a loved one or friend hooked, it's still incredibly hard to make sense of the madness. But the reality is, these thoughts and demands, internalised as the voice of a screaming bully, play out in day-to-day lives of many addicts. This is the first time I've ever put down in words my own "day in the life". Having just finished proof-reading this chapter the reality of the complete and utter madness I'm living in has literally smacked me in the face. I cannot continue to live like this!

CHAPTER 4
Clap for Carers

Beit a close loved one or simply a good friend, the impact from an experience desperately trying pull someone you care for from the depths of an addiction led crisis is not something that can be described in simple terms. It's traumatic, leaves long last scars, can break the most resilient of people, and doesn't carry the level of public awareness that it deserves.

Carers desperately want to see and support an addict in a journey that sees them revert back to the person they once knew. But all too often they too get caught up in the complex psychology that comes with addiction, left constantly on a knife edge, not knowing what to say or when to say it… because whatever they say will be wrong, running the risk of a backlash from their addiction possessed loved one/friend.

I love my wife with all my heart but will forever live with the guilt from what my experience with addiction put her through. She remains the caring, loving and funny women I met all those years ago, but whilst she'd never openly say it, the trauma my illness put her through has left deep scars. The same goes for my mum, a loving but sensitive lady in her 60's who should be relaxing in her retirement years rather than being left in highly anxious state witnessing her son battle with a degenerative eating disorder.

Put simply, whilst it's brutally unfair, the life of someone living with, or incredibly close to victim of addiction can be awful!

When Help Backfires

"Telling someone with depression to pull themselves together is about as useful as telling someone with cancer to just stop having cancer"

Ricky Gervais

I've lost count of the number of times when I was really ill that my wife or mum would desperately try to help me see sense by using words along the lines of "try to think about people who are less fortunate than you". This is a perfectly rational point to make when attempting to help someone in the midst of a mental health crisis see the reality that life could actually be a lot worse. But the reality is, if you're in the thick of a brutal battle with mental ill-health, despite the positive intent, this can be one of worst things someone could possibly say to you.

Battling with anxiety, depression, addiction, or any other form of mental illness doesn't strip one's awareness of darker side of the world today… young and old out there battling terminal illnesses, wealthy western democracies continue to allow people to sleep on the streets or live in overcrowded, poverty-stricken accommodation, and wars continue to rage resulting in countless innocent lives lost. The sad fact is a case of acute mental illness leaves its victim selfishly entrenched in their own mind, but at the same time, fully cognisant of the fact they've got so many things to be thankful for and wholly empathetic to the awful situation other less fortunate people face in this tough world.

Back in my darker days, when every part of my life had been consumed, I'd have swapped my life with an innocent child living in a war-torn country desperate for the chance to live. A bold statement which could lead to the conclusion that I'm making light of the plight of those living in warzones. The simple truth is that my headspace was in such a bad place that I honestly would have given someone else a chance to see and enjoy the positive side to life that I was blind to.

More often than not, where acute an addiction is present that seemingly rational and well-intended point made in a desperate attempt to help an addict see the positives in their life will trigger powerful emotions of guilt, self-loathing, and anger. "How the hell can you be sitting here freaking about the prospect of eating the two f*cking roast potatoes on your plate when kids out there starving... but unlike you, through no choice of their own? You must be the most self-centred, narcissist that's ever walked the earth".

It's a lose, lose situation for a carer, however you look at it!

Reassuring the Enemy

The phycological warfare encountered when simply trying nudge an addict onto a path to recovery often leaves them in constantly petrified of the backlash that comes their way should they say the wrong thing (which more often than not is right!). This fear can easily have a wholly unintentional consequence, with the carer inadvertently feeding the demands of underlying illness in a bid to keep the peace and therefore ensuring they feel safe.

Like most mums, my wife is a tough cookie and an absolute super mum in daily life, not that my kids are old, and therefore mature enough to truly recognise what she does for them... what our parents do for us becomes more apparent when we finally reach adulthood. Although she'd never admit to it, when I hit my lowest point, my illness had left her a broken woman inside, yet remarkably she remained strong enough to hide this from the eyes of our children. I was desperately trying to challenge what had become the dominant inner voice in my head demanding that I punish myself with increasing levels of calorific restriction and extreme exercise.... but the voice was too strong and would fight back, often in highly manipulative ways you would naturally expect. The extremely clever and devious attributes of my addiction would actually find ways to seek permission from my wife to engage in health destroying behaviours... to head out for another run or we should cancel the usual Saturday night takeaway as I didn't feel up to it (both wrong options).

Ultimately, I own my thoughts and actions, but as a beaten man, the illness had sapped every ounce of rational thinking capability from my mind. Words we're coming out of my mouth, but it was the illness talking to my wife... seeking permission to continue feeding (excuse the pun) a path to self-destruction. Already left mentally battered scarred by the experience of trying to support me and manage as a single parent, it's no wonder she was incapable of mustering any strength to respond with the assertiveness needed to stop me from doing what the voice was telling me to do. Instead, in a bid to secure some temporary respite from the trauma she too was experiencing, she'd naturally say "yes" to any request that came from my mouth. This would ultimately work to reinforce my behaviours.

Lies and Deceit

In the desperation that comes with a constant need to comply with the never ending "musts" that form the framework of an addiction, an addict will do just about anything to adhere to the demand. More often than not, this leads to secrecy and lies, both of which challenge even the strongest of relationships.

In today's world of manufactured online perfection, our ability to register the innate fallibility written in every strand of our human DNA is seemingly diminishing with each passing year... well, that's what I've observed. When it comes to me, I'm no different to anyone else. At work, I'd like to think that I'm an above average boss, but I recognise that I'm a little impatient at times. At home, my kids would say definitely say that I'm a strict dad... if only they knew what strict looked like! But on balance, whilst I have my faults, I hope the outside world sees me as a pretty good guy... loyal husband, father trying to help his children grow into respectable adults, empathetic boss, and someone who tries to give something back to their local community. In truth, I'm actually a pretty boring guy, which probably explains why I ended up becoming an accountant… process orientated, methodical, with an eye for detail… i.e. not the sort of guy to set a party alight. My biggest crime in life has been a couple of parking tickets, both of which left me f*cking infuriated!

I was brought up to hold honesty as a key component of my core value system, so I've never been one to hold secrets from people or tell lies… on the whole, what you see is what you get! But when living as a desperate addict, the eating disorder that had consumed every part of life had transformed me from being a trustworthy guy to a compulsive and highly deceitful liar… all in the interest of maintaining a degree of inner peace with my addiction.

Back in 2015, by then having reached breaking point, I'd regularly disappear from the house leaving my wife and kids at home with no knowledge of where I'd gone, only to return with an entirely believable but wholly fictitious story to explain my absence. I hadn't been down the pub for a couple of cheeky pints, I wasn't having a secret affair, and I hadn't taken the dog for a walk… because we didn't have one then! ☺. Instead, I'd have driven out and parked at the start of one my many rural running routes (where I wouldn't be seen) to smash out a hard and fast 10k run. The need to meet the overriding inner demand for movement, the same as the fix needed by a drug addict or alcoholic had become my number one priority in life.

I'll never forget the day when my wife caught me, guilty as sin! I'd gone out for one of my secret runs, only for one of her friends to spot me… I had no idea! When her friend innocently mentioned in passing that she'd seeing me out running I was quite rightly confronted, my wife seeking to validate if it was true after I'd told her I was elsewhere. In all honesty, I lied so many times back then that I've forgotten where the f*ck I'd said

I was going when I left the house. I'd been caught red handed, leaving me with no option but to tell her the truth. It's precisely this type of situation where an encounter with addiction can have a catastrophic and long-lasting impact on relationships. Trust takes years to build but can be destroyed within in the blink of an eye!

Empathetic Gratitude

I'm fully aware just how my illness affected those closest to me which has built a genuine level of empathy for anyone touched by the far-reaching effects of addiction. The fact is that carers are innocent bystanders, stood in the wrong place at the wrong time, witnessing a horrendous crime... but in these circumstances the criminal and victim are one of the same...a person whom they care deeply for.

Anyone with an ounce of compassion will always do their upmost to help someone suffering at the hands of an addiction to see the reality that they have to break the cycle. At the same time, the harsh reality is that the illness within will always hate anyone attempting to challenge its grip on the host it's consumed. All too often this leads to wholly uncharacteristic behaviours from a once loved one or friend, which can manifest in many different ways... lies, verbal aggression, physical abuse, and/or total isolation, all in an attempt to avoid anyone rightly attempting to challenge the addiction mindset. The sad truth is that all too often long-standing relationships are severed beyond repair as the intruder sat deep inside the victim finds ways to fight outside of the rule book in a bid to protect its host from any external influence.

If you're currently in the "firing line", desperately trying to help someone claw themselves out of the depths of an addiction, I'd urge you to direct your hate and anger towards the illness and not it's victim. Divorcing the addiction from the addict is bl**dy tough, especially when all you see in front of you is a someone you no longer recognise. But deep inside, an addict remains that person you remember with fondness. A combination of medication and therapy are critical to give an addict the chance of recovery, but it's the understanding, love, dedication and staying power of carers that make the real difference in helping to release the person they once knew.

And Finally

It's bl**dy hard to find the right words to articulate the sheer amount of personal gratitude I have for the support my 'carers' provided over the course of my own battle with addiction. My mum, stepdad and best mate Richard were always there for me in my times of need. But my biggest and heartfelt "thank you" goes to my amazing wife, who remained firmly by my side even when my journey towards recovery was treacherous and probably felt to her like a faraway place. She's one hell of a lady, far more resilient than she'd recognise in herself, carrying a true heart of gold!

HEALTH CHECK-IN

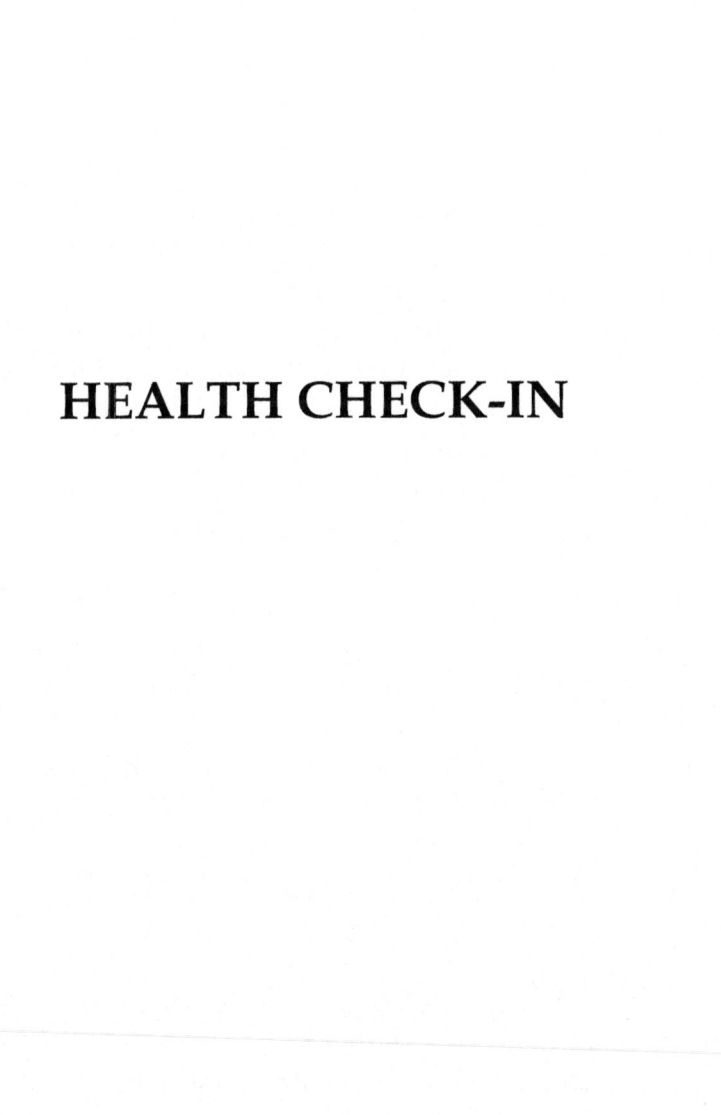

CHAPTER 5
73.0kg

As I stepped onto the scales this morning it dawned on me that it's been over a month since I last weighed myself, lightyears ahead of where I found myself a few years back. Then, I'd weigh myself up to 8 times a day (yep, that's every couple of hours folks), the seconds between stepping onto the scales and seeing the result representing the dividing line between a short period of contentment and complete meltdown. If the scales produced a reading just 0.1kg higher than my ever-reducing target weight being set by the controlling anorectic voice, all hell would break loose. Within an instant the inner voice would be chastising me, leaving me with painful self-loathing thoughts and in a volatile fight or flight state of mind… one totally harmless question from my wife would run the risk of being twisted by my then shrunken, malnourished brain, translating the words into some kind of criticism. This would provoke a backlash from my addiction, lashing out in defence of a totally non-existent threat. Looking back now I can't help but hate the person I became… but that person wasn't me!

At my lowest, my weight had plummeted to just 63kg. I'm 6'3" so at well under 10 stone there was little flesh left to spread over my extended body mass. If you've formed a mental image, it's more than likely to align with the reality. The best way I can articulate my physical state at the time would be a couple of levels up the health ladder from one of those disturbing charity appeals on TV pleading for donations to help get food to starving people in parts of the world besieged by famine and war.

Why would a guy, seemingly with everything to live for … married to a loving wife, father to two brilliant kids (most of the time!), decent job with a good salary, and living in a nice family home… end up in a state where he was bordering on starvation? The answer is simple… my body, mind and soul had been captured by an evil and highly unpredictable intruder, better known as Anorexia Nervosa.

Seven years have now been and gone since I was first diagnosed with an eating disorder. Having weighed myself this morning, the scales registering at 73kg, I'm now 10kg (22lb) heavier than I registered my lowest weight… that's a mere +1.43kg average gain per year. According to the NHS website, at 19.8, my BMI is now one of a perfectly healthy 44 year-old male specimen, although my wife would dispute the 'perfect specimen' ☺! For completeness the healthy BMI range sits between 18.5 and 25.0.

I find it staggering that according to our national health service, a fully grown man of my height and frame could be deemed 'healthy' at 67kg, a mere 4kg more than the point I'd reached physical breaking point back (67kg would give me a BMI of 18.5). Having reached 73kg, it will come as no surprise that I feel significantly healthier, stronger and more energised today … but… my body and mind are yet to have the essential resilience needed to respond in a rational way to some of the more testing demands of daily life. I can categorically say that back when I had managed to put on the 4kg needed from the lowest point to reach the 67kg, which put me into the green BMI zone, every part of my life remained utterly f*cked!

What does support to recover from anorexia look like today in the UK?

Firstly, like all treatable but debilitating illnesses, the best chance of recovery comes with an early diagnosis! It's now become a taboo to publicly criticise NHS, which has developed a godly like status since the pan smashing Thursdays during pandemic. But I'll buck the trend by stating that when it comes to the science that sits behind the diagnosis of eating disorders, the NHS has moved on little since the 1980's. GPs still continue to view eating disorders like anorexia nervosa through the prism of physical health, using BMI as the primary means to decipher whether a red flag is raised. This in itself can hamper any chance of an early diagnosis and triage into the appropriate treat treatment pathway should you turn up to your doctors with a BMI of 25, yet psychologically displaying all the hallmarks of the early stages of an anorectic mindset.

The other area in which anorectics are being failed by the health services is when it comes to being considered for in-patient treatment. I've heard varying stories concerning the BMI that someone needs to present with to be classified as 'high risk', but they all point to somewhere around 15. The sad reality is that we're increasingly seeing cases where a patient's BMI has fallen significantly below 15 before they've been given a chance to secure in-patient care. I don't blame the NHS for this issue as the expediential growth we've seen in eating disorder cases being presented is now lightyears above the funding and infrastructure in place to treat demand. To give you a sense of what a sub 15 BMI looks like, I stand just shy of 2 metres tall and would weigh less than 55kg/8.6 stone... i.e., nothing but skin and bone. The simple fact is that body mass index was never meant to be a measure of overall physical or mental health. But this rudimentary measure continues to be used when patients present with the early or even developed stages of complex mental health conditions.

Over the last 20 years of working most of my jobs have come with a staff benefit in the form of company paid private health insurance. Given past experiences with public sector health, I never take this for granted, knowing that it gives me to the same private healthcare as the customers who pay for their own medical cover. If needed, I could access out or inpatient care within days of a GP referral. Without this safety net the likelihood is that I'd have limited, if any support from the NHS if my circumstances took a turn for the worse again. Long ago, I did spend some time in NHS outpatient treatment services but was discharged from the West Sussex eating disorder support services at the start of the pandemic. At that time my BMI had reached the NHS benchmark (18.5), but the reality was that I was far from healthy. At the point when I was discharged, just like so many others in my situation, I wasn't physically at risk. I was just about able to function, but still far from reaching a good state of health.

The fact is that whilst weight gain is essential to deliver a healthier state of cognitive function, the highly addictive nature of illnesses like anorexia means those affected have far a longer and arduous journey to finally reach the point of recovery. If I'm being brutally honest, as things stand right now, after 7 years battling against this illness, I simply don't know whether it's possible that I could actually reach the point of 'self-actualising' freedom from this illness that I yearn. I'm able to function in day-to-day life but after such an extended period since my initial diagnosis, I've grown increasingly tired of waiting for the day to come when I wake up feeling alive once again.

Experiences battling an eating disorder or other forms of addiction can go on for decades. Some addicts, like myself, manage to navigate out of the danger zone to a functioning state but this is only halfway in the journey to freedom. All too often, people only ever reach the midpoint between the ground and the summit of the recovery mountain. I now need to find strength from within to give it one last final push.

I know the strong anorexic compulsions and controls will fight back, just like a cornered cat, hissing violently, teeth visible, back arched and claws fully extended. I live in hope that the power of writing will help me battle against these inevitable withdrawal symptoms.

CHAPTER 6
The Medical

Today saw my long awaited medical 'MOT' appointment finally arrive... four hours of prodding and poking (questioning and physically), needles, fitness tests, and of course the test that despite its importance, most men over the age of 40 dread the thought of. Don't worry, no intention to go into any detail on that front ☺! The company I work for offer it to all over 40's and despite the dreaded 'man' test and having to venture into the delight that is Crawley for the test, I'm eager to find out if the last 7 years living with an eating disorder has left my health unscathed or in some way left some permanent physical scares.

On completion of the usual pre-medical questionnaire a couple of days ago, focused on answering the usual lifestyle, diet, exercise, and alcohol consumption questions, I came across the condition that that I'm to arrive at the appointment 'nil by mouth' for at least 10 hours... required to ensure that blood results aren't skewed by spikes in blood sugar or caffeine. The problem is my appointment is at 12:30, meaning the last time I'm allowed to eat will when my wife and I sit down to eat dinner the night before... having dealt with the usual teenage squabbles.

Asking a recovering anorexic to starve themselves, even for a short period of time, is like asking a recovering alcoholic to have a beer, just the one, then forget you ever had it. Granted, my illness is far less dominant than it was in the past, but the thought of starving myself for 15 hours struck an element of fear from within... fear this could allow the remaining elements of my addict wired mind to reconnect and build enough strength to weaken the loose control I currently have over it. Sound a little over dramatic? A single alcoholic drink for someone 'on the wagon' is deemed a relapse, carrying risk that dormant addiction receptors in the brain will drive an intense thirst for more. It's no different if a recovering anorectic skips a meal, potentially allowing those receptors to reconnect with the false euphoria from starvation. I've climbed a number of steps up the recovery ladder to finally a functioning state, so I'm left nervous of landing on a snake that takes me all the way back to square one on the board.

I just about manage to get through the morning without eating, but my 'healthy' BMI hides what continues to be an under-nourished body with little to no reserves left in the tank. By midday, my stomach literally feels like it's starting to digest itself, but I guess there's a sense of relief I should take that my brain is actually telling me to nourish myself.

Arriving at the health centre I'm greeted by a physiologist who sits me down and asks a series of questions …are you feeling well today? any allergies? fear of needles? how much alcohol to you consume? any medical history to be aware of? "Hmmm, let me think… oh yeah a long history of mental illness coupled with an addiction to starvation" … sarcasm is my only way to feel a sense of light relief within the madness over recent years.

Blood samples are taken first, then urine (why are the sample pots so f*cking small?), followed by height and waist measurements, blood pressure check, ECG following a dry chest shave, strength & flexibility tests (you try touching your f*cking toes when you've got a 35" inside leg) ... and finally, the weigh in! …73.2kg. Samples are then taken to the onsite laboratory for testing (I hope they wore gloves when handling the pee pot! ☺).

1pm arrives and I finally get to sit down and eat something, smashing through a banana, apple, and two cereal bars like I've not eaten for a week! I'm then invited back into the examination room by a physiologist to run through my test results produced by the medical software algorithm. With exception of my alcohol consumption which at 35 units a week, double the limit set by public health England, I'm a perfect specimen of health ...good diet, regular exercise, healthy waistline, and a BMI at 20. Justification to avoid making any changes to the way I currently live (with exception of cutting out red wine)? Certainly not, so I politely challenge the practitioner on the false reality the algorithm has given compared to my real state of health.

The second hour is spent with a private GP running through my blood and urine test results and the dreaded testicle and prostate examinations, neither of which prove to be anywhere near as bad as my male pride had feared. My blood and urine results are pretty much bang on perfection. Despite my 'A*' liver function results, the expected challenge about weekly alcohol consumption duly followed. Having witnessed alcoholism destroy both my dad and grandad's lives, I know there's absolutely zero chance that I could follow the same path. I end up giving the GP the usual false promise to cut down having already decided to exercise my right to bodily autonomy.

Finally, I'm back in with the physiologist again for lung strength and capacity tests and full assessment of my overall fitness. The fitness test based on assessing my Vo2 max involved cycling on an exercise bike with my chest strapped up to an ECG monitor. The test starts at an easy pace and from there the speed and intensity are increased every minute. Unsurprisingly I breeze through the test delivering a result that put my fitness in in the top 10 percent for my age group.

The day finishes with an 'health age' report, providing an assessment of my all-round body age to compare with my actual age. I'm given a health age of 36, 7 years lower than my actual years. After years of simultaneously pounding myself and starving my body of vital nourishment I'm relieved to hear no obvious signs of any long lasting damage to my physical health. But the glowing health report I'm given is far from reflective of the way I actually feel within. I still carry an exhausted body and a mind imprisoned by the remains of a hidden inner enemy that even the most sophisticated of algorithms would have no way of detecting.

THE UK ADDICTION CRISIS

HEALTH & CHARITY SECTORS
+
THE 'BREADWINNERS' SECRET

CHAPTER 7
The UK Health Sector

I'll start this chapter with a promise not to bore you with any more rants about the continued use of BMI by GPs to diagnose and/or decipher the extent to which an anorectic needs medical support... It's not one to forget but I recognise that the point was rammed home in Chapter 5.

Whilst acknowledging that eating disorders only form a small slice of a large and growing pie representing the number of addiction related illnesses out there, it's the area I'm most informed to write about with a degree of credibility, including the subject of how the NHS treats these conditions. That said, it doesn't take a f*cking rocket scientist to join the dots between the widely publicised UK mental health crisis and all-round failure of public health services to treat the most vulnerable, to conclude that all NHS addiction treatment services are in the same state as those focused on eating disorders.... failing the very patients that services are in place to support!

Top of my list when it comes to personal bug bears about public health is one that the NHS itself can take zero responsibility for... our vital public health service being used as a political weapon! The NHS has always been a political hot potato, but its politicisation reached record heights during the pandemic, with government lockdowns enforced on the basis that it would save the service. This lifted our public health service to a saint like status, worshiped by the entire nation as we stood outside at 8pm every Thursday evening clapping in gratitude... us Brits are f*cking weird at times!

Whilst the pandemic period saw the politicisation of the NHS reach its peak, its status as Westminster hot potato stems back way before the pandemic. In truth, the level of toxicity in the NHS debate had been growing ever since austerity measures were first introduced in a bid to balance the books following the world economic crash back in 2007. Ever since then the dividing line on the political battleground has sat between the left who cite under-funding as the only cause of the crisis in NHS services, and the right, who point the finger firmly at public service inefficiency. In truth, we all know that a mix of both arguments are to blame, but what really 'gets my goat' is that politicians from all sides are blind to this, continuing a narrative of conflict which only serves to halt the corrective action desperately needed. When it comes to mental health services, the constant focus on political point scoring rather than both sides working together to actually address the issues is doing nothing more than leave some of the most vulnerable people in our society sat on the side-line waiting for the help they desperately need. At the same time front-line psych health professionals are left in the demoralising position where despite doing their very best every day, they see patient after patient failed by the system.

From my own personal experience under the care of the NHS, its eating disorder treatment services are now way beyond breaking point. Services simply cannot cope with the increasing demand driven by a combination in an ever-rising number of cases being presented and changes in the complexity of cases being presented. Long standing treatment techniques, used for decades, have become outdated and struggling to cope with how elements of the increasingly complex world we live in have started to alter how conditions are manifesting.

Outside of a handful of medical specialists in the in the field of eating disorders, few will recognise that a vastly different approach is needed than that prescribed to cure other forms of addiction. The foundation for the successful treatment of alcohol, drug or gambling addiction is built on the concept of complete abstinence from the addictive draw... with no return, ever! Eating disorders, especially in those like anorexia nervosa which often manifests through an addiction to starvation coupled with extreme levels of exercise, are significantly more complex to treat. When it comes to anorexia, you can't simply abstain from the behaviours at the centre of the condition. Afterall, when it comes to starvation, the patient has already become addicted to abstinence! The approach needed is more subtle and is inherently more complex, dependent on turning up the dial on one element of the addiction (by refeeding the body) and turning it down on the other element (exercise)... this proves overwhelmingly complex for an addict to process and act upon when their already malnourished brain is capable of little more than continuing to the behaviours demanded by an entrenched pattern of thinking I'd say that 9 out of 10 therapists will always advise from the outset that a patient must stop exercising immediately. Perfectly sound and logical advice given the circumstances, but speaking from my own experience, some exercise is vital in recovery to stimulate the cognitive strength needed fight the fight. I know I'll be chastised by many in the medical profession for going against the grain of the standard approach to treat anorexia, but my view is that complete abstinence from any form of strenuous exercise often proves to be totally counterproductive... unless of course, the condition has advanced to a stage where it threatens a patient's very existence.

My overwhelming experience with NHS GP services over the years has illustrated a significant knowledge gap when it comes to their ability to spot the onset of an eating disorder versus more general mental health conditions (e.g., anxiety). GPs aren't expected to be experts, hence the 'General' in their title, but arguably, an early diagnosis when it comes to eating disorders carries is of equal importance to catching cancer early. Afterall, anorexia nervosa carries the highest mortality rate across a broad spectrum of mental illnesses. It's a sad fact that in many cases patients end up being triaged into more generalised forms mental health treatment which aren't sophisticated enough to stem the flow of the underlying illness. Before you think that as a medically untrained accountant I'm having a cheap shot at NHS GPs, I should state for the record that I actually carry a great deal of sympathy for them. Whilst the condescending undertone that I've regularly encountered from some GPs has felt far from best practice, they're all hampered by an overwhelming demand for their time. Afterall, appointment times have been slashed to a maximum of 10 minutes… a window of time wholly insufficient to stand any chance of spotting an emerging complex mental health issue. The situation today is a long way from when I was a kid. Back in the 80's a GP would see you for as long as it took to get to the bottom of the problem. These days GPs are literally being handed a Rubix Cube they have to solve in a matter of minutes every time a patient walks through the door.

It's no wonder that a 10-minute diagnosis window usually ends up with patients presenting the early signs of an eating disorder often leaving with a month's supply of antidepressants, and if incredibly lucky, an onward referral into local, more generalised mental health support services… with a 6-12 month wait to actually see anyone. Personally, I don't care whether the blame for the broken state of public health services sits with mismanagement within the NHS or in central government. What I do care about is the need for all parties carrying an element of accountability in this debate have to start realising is that you can't simply paper over the initial cracks in the early stages of addiction with a course of Prozac and access to online CBT training. Yet if you present yourself to your GP with a suspicious lump, the chances are that you'll be referred for an urgent biopsy, receive an accurate diagnosis and if needed triaged into treatment. Pre pandemic, when things were bad but not as bad as now, beginning to end, this would have probably taken about a month. I just don't get why mental ill-health continues to be viewed as a second-tier priority to physical health when it comes to the allocation of NHS resources?

Back in 2015, shortly after my diagnosis, I was referred into the

Sussex eating disorder outpatient services. At that stage, carrying a body and mind utterly f*cked by anorexia, I'd only been living with the condition for 6 months, creating an expectation this was a golden ticket that would see a swift return to normality for me and my family… 7 years on, it's fair to say the reality turned out to be far from that expected. I recall that first appointment like it was only yesterday, a community-based practitioner visiting my wife and I in the January of 2015… nice lady, but clearly overworked, leaving the distinct impression that her heavily restricted bandwidth restricted her ability to deliver the standards of care she strived to provide. The session started with me providing a detailed account of my daily diet and exercise regime…. at that point, 1500 calories consumed / 3000 calories burnt. At this stage in my journey my addiction had firmly attached itself to every part of my life, with all the evidence pointing towards a continued deterioration in both my physical and mental state. So, I was dumbfounded when the practitioner left the house having given me the following plan of action:

1. Stop **all** exercise… immediately!

2. Consume a **minimum** of 3500 calories per day… immediately!

I mean, for f*ck sake, does it really require years of medical training to come up with a plan of action that my 4-year-old son (at the time) could have formed. Anyone with an ounce of common sense, especially my wife at the time, could see that whilst the plan was entirely logical, there's a reality to case of addiction that didn't correlate with the advice I'd been given… try walking into your local pub at 11am and head to the guy who's sat at the same table all day every day and suggest he stops drinking immediately… I'm sure we will all come up with the likely response!

In an acute case of addiction, the overwhelming need for a medicinal hit to sooth the inner pain, be that endorphins, alcohol, or drugs, will always carry a far greater power than an addict's own self-interest. In my case, the perfectly sound advice I received, which to be frank I already knew, was never going to turn my head away from an addiction that'd become all consuming. Determination is definitely not something that I lack in daily life, but self-will alone was never going to drag me out of the hole I found myself in.

Having failed to secure the complex help I genuinely needed through the NHS, I resorted to my work funded private health insurance. You'd naturally think that access to private healthcare will always result in a patient receiving the very best standard of care, but my experience back in 2015 proved that money and higher standards don't always come hand in hand when it comes to private sector health.

I was referred to a consultant psychiatrist based in Kent; someone I'd desperately like to name but I fear potential legal consequences given the status he holds as a professional who spent decades working at some of the best hospitals specialising in treating eating disorders. I'll never forget his rather grand home in the Kent countryside where he'd see his patients, clearly worth well in excess of a million, which only went to reinforce my perception that I was in the care of safe and highly experienced hands. How wrong was I?

At the end of my second appointment the consultant prescribed 400mg of Pregabalin per day, which over the course of the following weeks was increased to 600mg, then to 750mg, and ultimately to 900mg. I didn't have a clue what I was taking, taking it on face value that this guy knew what he was doing. It was probably a year later having done my homework that I found out that Pregabalin is a drug more commonly used to treat neuropathic pain, epilepsy and nerve pain issues associated with diabetes. Whilst it can be used in the treatment of psychological conditions, it's uncommon owing it's highly addictive nature. I found myself in a situation where I was not only addicted to the behaviours that anorexia demanded of me, but I was now a full blown addict of a prescription drug given to me by a private consultant who made no attempt to warn me of the potential consequences. Pregabalin would once again turn my world upside down in 2020!

Having finally realised that despite his experience, the consultant psychiatrist had done little to help me address any aspect of my eating disorder, I left his so called 'care' in 2016. If anything, I'd say my condition actually deteriorated under his care. In shear desperation I reverted back to the NHS, but despite raised eyebrows from my GP when I told them how much Pregabalin I was taking each day, they continued to prescribe the 900mg daily dosage. It took a further three years for an NHS psychiatrist to outwardly display her disgust that I had been taking such a high dosage of Pregabalin such a long period. At the time she informed me that medical guidelines stipulated a maximum dose of 600mg can be prescribed, but only for serious cases of epilepsy.

Addiction to Pregabalin

"Addiction can occur after a spell of legitimate prescription use, especially when your body gets used to it. Recreational users also see the drug as a means to get 'high' and enjoy sensations of pleasure it creates"

addictionhelper.com

When Pregabalin is prescribed over a long period the body builds a tolerance and dependency to this powerful drug. The drugs strong withdrawal symptoms act as a motivation to keep taking the drug, which could go some way to explain why street level demand for this medication has risen sharply over recent years (it's a Class C controlled substance). For patients with a history of anxiety and depression, withdrawal effects can worsen when the drug is stopped abruptly. It's also known that prescribing Pregabalin to people with a history of addiction carried a considerable risk of extending their addiction to the medication.

So why the f*ck would a psychiatrist with years of experience treating patients with eating disorders, with full knowledge of the addictive nature of conditions like anorexia, prescribe me with a drug he knew full well would run the risk of adding another string to my addiction bow? I sometimes think about making a retrospective formal complaint concerning what would probably be deemed as patient neglect when I was under the care of the consultant. But what good would it do? Yes, it could lead to well-deserved justice, but it would be painful and most likely serve as a complete distraction from the focus I need to finally say goodbye to anorexia.

In truth, I've no conscious recollection of pregabalin ever giving me a sense of euphoria to help to distract me from my primary challenge presented by my eating disorder. Nor did my body or mind give me any indication that I'd become reliant on the medication. I ended up taking it for 5 years without a single question from my doctor, the monthly online repeat prescription request allowing me to bypass the challenge as he focused on dealing with the demand from patients being seen in person. This was until a chance encounter with an NHS psychiatrist who told me in no uncertain terms that I needed to stop taking it immediately.

My Pregabalin detox started in the summer of 2020. With a global pandemic dominating every element of our lives it was hardly the time of balance and tranquility needed to tackle a drug addiction. I had no idea what would happen, and being brutally honest, I was way too blasé at the start about the challenge that lie ahead.

CHAPTER 8
Detox

Being completely oblivious to the scale of the challenge that lay ahead of me, my detox plan looked pretty easy on paper, a steady reduction from 900mg of Pregabalin each day to zero in fortnightly incremental drops of 50mg. I recall at the time thinking "F*ck, that's 36 weeks!. Surely it can't be that hard, I'll be done within 20 weeks… max!?".

The reality turned out to be a detox journey that ultimately would take pretty much the whole of 2020. Yes, the year everyone would prefer to forget about, but at the risk of coming across as a complete narcissist, dealing with the heavily restricted life and parental burden given to us by the pandemic gave us felt like a stroll in the park compared to a year of Pregabalin detox. The determination and grit that form an intrinsic part my DNA remained as strong as ever, but at times the pain was indescribable, simultaneously battling with the harsh withdrawal pangs whilst desperately trying to continue functioning as a husband, father, son, and employee.

I'd absolutely dread that fortnightly alarm bell signaling the need to drop the dosage by another increment, knowing it would lead to another 4-5 days of shivers, aches, heightened anxiety, panic attacks and heart palpitations. Even worse, was the overwhelming urge I had to revert back to anorectic behaviours in a bid to give a sense of control. I craved intense exercise to the extent that I was capable of causing harm to anyone who got in my way. With pandemic restrictions at the time preventing me from accessing the local swimming pool, the worst case scenario started to unfold. I found myself slipping back into the old routine of running up to 10 miles every day for weeks on end. This saw all of the f*cking hard work I'd ploughed in over the 5 preceding years near enough evaporate, as half of the 10kg I'd gained would disappear in only a handful of months.

The withdrawal symptoms got significantly harder to cope with after the first 3 months, with the 50mg reduction becoming an ever-higher -proportion of the daily dosage I'd been taking the previous fortnight. By the time my dosage had dropped to 250mg the very thought of reducing it by a 20% (50mg) overnight meant a conversation with my GP became essential. My body and mind had been left waving a white flag which thankfully my GP could see, duly agreeing to drop the fortnightly reduction from there on to a more manageable 25mg.

Over what felt like 12 long and hard months spanning 2020 I received an unquestionable level of support from my wife and mum. Without this, I'd question whether could have successfully weaned myself off the medication. The ironic thing is that despite the impact that the experience of detoxing had on me, my stereotypical and highly proud alpha male mindset meant the turmoil I was going through was never detected by anyone else, especially when it came to my professional life… an approach I wouldn't recommend to anyone else living through similar circumstances. Stiff upper lip syndrome stopped me from uttering a single word about my dilemma to my very understandable boss about, instead, choosing to navigate through the challenge without taking a single day off at work, letting any of my deliverables slip, or leaving my colleagues with any sense of what I was going through.

Eventually I won my battle against Pregabalin, but I'm far from proud of the way I went about it. Hindsight tells me that I should have been more open with by boss, just as I'd been with my wife and mum. My experience working with him tells me that he would have understood, giving me some essential time out…. without any consequences on my career prospects. Whilst the world is far more understanding of these types of challenges than ever before, the biggest challenge faced by guys like me is more often than not us!

CHAPTER 9
The UK Charity Sector

Our world has gone through more change in the last 20 years than the entire preceding century, largely driven by the growing influence of tech across every aspect of daily life. I'm not stupid enough (although my mates would argue otherwise) to solely blame the likes of tech giants like Apple and Google for facilitating the mental health crisis the western world currently finds itself in. At the same time, you'd be hard pushed to argue against the view that tech has without doubt played its part in creating and fueling the problem. When it comes to the impact it's had on characteristically addiction led illnesses, there's no doubt that tech has added a whole new level of complexity for both support services and addicts themselves to try and navigate through.

It's an unquestionable fact that both government and private medical sector CEOs have failed miserably over the last decade to invest adequately in medically led digital capability to help manage the ever-increasing level of demand and complexity across the mental health landscape. This won't have been a conscious decision, but nonetheless likely to have been a big miscalculation from both sides. But why haven't they invested sooner? In the public sector it's simply not been a priority, partly down to the taboo associated with mental illness, which has kept a tight lid on the subject for decades, thereby leaving the masses unexposed to the problem... a lid that finally cracked open when the pandemic hit. In the private sector, it's been more a case of lacking the essential, compelling business case to justify significant levels of digital investment in a sector where the commercial benefits have been hard to forecast. Put simply, until more recently when the surge in demand has finally opened up the eyes of CEOs to the opportunity, I suspect that many of them remained highly sceptical about the earning power from mental health to meet the returns required by shareholders. Private sector investment has been late coming, but with the £ and $ signs now clear for any CEO to see, huge amounts are now being invested in the mental health tech space.

As I sit here in 2022, the public sector continues to fail miserably and whilst it's probably working on it, the private sector is yet to develop a magical bullet to move the dial in support for those with addiction led mental illnesses. So where have addicts been going in an attempt to seek the right type of support they desperately need? Increasingly, they've been resorting to the charity sector in search of help, which often only happens once they've reached crisis point. An important additional point to note, which I'll dig deeper into later on is the huge disparity between the level of charity led support available to addicts, which varies depending on the type of addiction someone has.

I've long had concerns about the vast salaries that some charity CEOs receive, which has never sat right with me. But I've nothing but admiration for the frontline workers in this sector where the financial rewards are notably poor but the opportunity to build personal self-worth is usually there in abundance. There are some brilliant causes out there each with volunteers and poorly paid employees who give everything they've got, working incredibly hard to fill in the gaps in service that our hard-earned taxes should be delivering for us.

Charity Funding

There are two primary factors that usually determine the level of support available to someone seeking charity led assistance in a bid to tackle addiction:

Location

Where you live matters! Just as we saw the pandemic change the way many of us work overnight, moving traditional office-based jobs to hybrid/home working arrangements, it's also helped change the way therapy can be delivered. Remote therapy has undoubtably lifted the bar, providing greater access to services for those living in more remote locations… but just as we've seen in broader work settings where people are being asked to return to the office, therapy via Zoom will never come close to the power of a conversation in person.

Where you live has absolutely no bearing on your chance of one day forming a relationship with addiction. But it's clear, if you live outside of the city centres, unable to wait for public or afford the high cost associated with private therapy, the chances are that you'll also be left struggling to access charity services.

Aside from the huge salaries some charity CEOs earn, one thing they all have in common is the need to deploy resource where it can have the greatest benefit to achieve their purpose. Unsurprisingly this is usually concentrated where the masses live, leaving people distant from city centres lacking options to seek help.

I live in East Grinstead, a medium to large sized town in West Sussex… three supermarkets, leisure centre, small cinema, countless pubs and restaurants, and a train service straight into London in an hour… in my mind hardly remote! A few years back, when I'd reached a state of desperation, I finally swallowed my male pride and reached out to an eating disorder charity for help. But the nearest support group for men required a 2.5 hour round trip to Brighton.

I attended one session down in Brighton, and whilst the support was great, it wasn't something I could commit to, largely down to the demands of work. Sound like a convenient excuse? In truth, there's some weight behind that argument… when ill, an addict will always find an excuse to avoid being exposed to a challenge aimed at their addiction. But at the same time, the concept of hybrid working didn't exist then, creating a genuine risk of career limiting damage attached to being away from my London based office once a week… it's not right, but it's the way it was in my line of work back then.

Type of Addiction

The disparity is vast between the level of charity support available for different forms of addiction. There's an AA (Alcoholics Anonymous) group in every city and most towns across the UK. The same can't be said when it comes to accessing support groups for people attached to 'niche' forms of addiction.

I've looked into this a little, selecting sex as a recognised form of addiction we'd all consider to be at the 'taboo' end of the addiction scale (so, no wise cracks please!). At the time of writing, in March 2022, there are only 20 therapy groups run by Sexaholics Anonymous across the whole of the UK. This compares to 4661 UK based meetings run AA. An addiction to sex, which I'm guessing would also include online porn (?) is a genuine and growing issue, but I'd think that good old British frigidness makes it an awkward subject matter to raise awareness and from there secure appropriate levels of funding support. Afterall, how many people have you seen on the TV running the London marathon, with Sexaholics Anonymous plastered across their technical running vest? Yes, I am allowing my humour to get the better of me, possibly stepping over the mark, but the point I'm trying to make is actually a serious one. I've no doubt that charities like Sexaholics Anonymous provide an equally critical lifeline to those accessing their services as those using AA. That said, whilst I'd never expect there to be fund raising parity between these two charities, I strongly suspect that the funding gap between the two is wholly disproportionate to the scale of scale of demand they're both trying to service.

Like it or not, the fact is that both a lack of awareness and the extent to which society accepts the existence of some forms of addiction can result in charities falling way short of the funds they actually need to service the demand at their door. As an attempt to illustrate, in spite of the clear public awareness that exists concerning the escalating number of people living with eating disorders in the UK, 'Beat' which is probably the UK's largest eating disorder charity raised £3.3m in 2021. A solid effort but a mere just 10% of the amount raised by 'Gambleaware".

The charity I reached out to back in 2015, attending a solitary group session, was 'MGEDT' (Men Get Eating Disorders Too). I didn't stay in contact with them, a decision I later went on to regret, knowing benefit I'd have got by continuing access the company of like-minded guys who were facing / faced similar issues. Having recently tried to access the MGET website I was left disappointed to find the domain no longer in use, pointing to an outcome that the charity had folded. Sam Thomas, the founding member of MGET who'd suffered at the hands of Bulimia, also chaired the group meeting I attended. He was a visibly passionate guy, clearly wanting to help other men also caught up in a life using their nutritional intake as an unhealthy means to cope with life. Having run a google search on Sam's name I found out that the guy who had the inspiration to set up MGET in a bid to help others had ultimately gone on to develop an unhealthy relationship with alcohol:

"'I relapsed in a different way,' I explain to people about my transition from bulimia to alcohol addiction. We need to acknowledge this crossover rather than think conditions are in neat & tidy boxes. Otherwise we're in danger of switching one for another"

Sam Thomas

Later on in Sam's Twitter/X feed there was a suggestion that he was now clean, but clearly still doing his best to raise awareness on the subject of addiction.

So where is MGET today? From my research the charity appears be operating under a new name, "Male Voice ED". I've not reached out to them but I'm sure they're continuing to try and support guys in this field as best as possible, but having looked at their registered accounts, probably not to the extent they would like to. In 2021 Male Voice ED raised a mere £42,000 in funds which proved to be somewhat of a bitter pill for me to swallow!

Sam Thomas' point concerning the way different forms of addiction are packaged into "neat & tidy boxes" hit the nail right on the head for me. Whilst there are subtle differences between the way different forms of addiction can manifest, the underlying illness is largely the same. This leads me to imagine a world where all the addiction focused charities come together to form a powerhouse of good causes supporting the fight against the illness. The sum of all those parts, funding, expertise, lobbying power, and resource, working for one overarching cause, could achieve so much more. Until we see the mindset shift away from packaging different forms of addiction to looking at the problem more holistically, the likelihood of anything changing is slim.

Regulation

As the chief regulator of the gambling industry the Gambling Commission's mission is to keep crime out of gambling, to ensure that gambling is conducted fairly and openly, and to protect children and vulnerable people. GambleAware is a registered charity forming an independent subset of industry regulation via a framework agreement with the regulator to deliver a national strategy to reduce gambling harm. It's also funded by the bookmakers that form the industry!

You cannot miss the constant flow of cleverly advertised warnings across all media platforms about the risks associated with gambling, clever in the sense they probably ending up working to encourage gambling rather than act as a deterrent. Advertising noticeably ramps up when the weekend arrives, coinciding with the usual packed schedule of professional sport, and over a solid month when the 2-year cycle of World Cups and Euros land, presenting a bumper jackpot opportunity for the bookies. With more profit than ever to be made out of gambling (not by the punter) why do we continue to be drawn into a false sense of security that bookmakers genuinely give a f*ck about the GambleAware ethos they fund… 'when the fun stops, stop!'?

The conflict of interest is visible for all to see… encouraging people to stop gambling, including the 'problem' gamblers, conflicts with the core principle at the centre of the capitalised world we live in… the freedom of choice. Asking a business to genuinely buy into the principle of restricting its profits runs into direct conflict with its primary purpose… to maximise shareholder value. The gambling industry as a whole and the individual companies that form it are no different to us humans… to survive and if lucky, prosper, they must continuously adapt to the ever-changing environment they operate in. The fact that the very nature of addiction means that 'problem' gamblers aren't able to make a rational decision to stop when an advert tells them to, is of absolutely no concern to the bookies.

My broader take on this subject is that from a commercial perspective, the gambling industry has clearly adapted remarkably well to regulation, turning a business risk into a massive opportunity. They've exploited the valuable marketing collateral from fronting their business with the socially responsible 'shop window' their association with GambleAware provides. A desire to sustain or grow the number of 'problem' gamblers will never appear in any documented gambling industry goals, but consciously or subconsciously, the industry and the shareholders that fund it have formed their own addiction to the business earnings created by people willing to bet their life away. This makes it farcical that responsibility for funding and owning the delivery of messages about the issue of gambling addiction has been handed to the regulated.

If the last paragraph left you thinking "what the f*ck is the guy on about?", think about it like this... Bookies themselves are put in charge of delivering the message "when the fun stops, stop!" which sits on the very advertising aimed at promoting gambling. At the same time, they pay top dollar sporting celebrities to deliver the message. Ever thought that for 'problem' gamblers this creates a reverse psychological impact? The socially responsible image created by the bookie using one of their sporting heroes to spread the word works to make the 'problem' customer feel even safer in their hands.

So, has the ore of safety created by the gambling industry being left to sell the image of corporate social responsibility actually contributed to the growing problem of gambling addiction? In truth it's an impossible question to answer with any science. I've spent years working in private sector commercial finance jobs which makes me pretty sure that bookmakers would have missed a big trick if they're yet to establish a monetised interested in using the corporate responsibility that comes with an association to GambleAware.

You'd be forgiven for thinking that I'm starting to sound like Jeremy Corbin on the main stage at Glastonbury, ranting about the ills of a free market economy. To set the record straight I'm a true capitalist at heart, but years of experience working in the private sector does form a view that regulation structured in this way (i.e., where the regulated fund the regulator) will never work to successfully achieve it's intended outcome... in this case, to stem the rise in cases of gambling addiction.

Glossy magazines that pummel society via print and online distribution depicting the vision of a utopian body and life don't carry the same marketing advantage that benefits the gambling sector (i.e., 'good cause' association). You know the type of publications I'm referring to… the ones that sell us the dream that you'll be rewarded with the perfect six pack within a month if you simply follow a series of prescribed steps… although ironically, a slightly different programme for perfection does tend to appear \in every edition … or convincing us that the celery shake diet is a genuinely better alternative to a balanced routine of healthy nutrition and exercise in a bid to shed the 10lb needed to fit into that party dress!

So, why doesn't the same opportunity exist for these companies? It's quite simple… there's absolutely no incentive for the government to regulate them with mandatory warnings about the potential dangers associated with diet plans that any sensible GP would dis-credit, or normalising a false representation of the average human body. Over the last 2-3 decades the UK has developed the same obesity epidemic as that being experienced by our cousins across the Atlantic. At this moment cue the age-old saying … "when the US sneezes, the UK catches a cold"! Put simply, what incentive is there for the government regulate sections of the media selling an obsession with exercise and weight loss in a bid to achieve bodily perfection… even if a link exists between what they publish and the onset of eating disorders. Afterall, the very heart of the messaging is more than likely to be viewed by the government as an enabler to help improve public health, thereby saving the NHS millions from the increasing pot of money spent dealing with obesity.

Maybe this is why regulations around the gambling sector are seemingly weak… why adopt the type of tough regulation actually needed to help prevent harm when the industry has an annual worth reported at £14 billion, generating huge revenues for the exchequer?

Maybe I'm just a synic... in fact I know I am... but this is the way I read the situation!

Government Lobbying... "Money Talks"

Long, long ago when I studied A Level Politics, I developed a keen interest in all things Westminster, which I've held until more recently (I'll explain why in chapter 17). My wife who carries absolutely zero interest in politics has mastered the art of mindfulness over the years, removing her mind and soul from the living room at 10pm every night when I begin ranting at Hu Edwards presenting the 10 o'clock news... Note to reader... my reference to Hu Edwards was written pre scandal. I thought about supplementing with an immature wisecrack but concluded that it would be an ill-advised move ☺.

Later in the book I'll touch on my views concerning the broader societal impact I see associated with Political scandals. For now, I'll keep it be brief and on script with this chapter's theme... The consistent flow of scandals we've witnessed in British politics over recent years has not only left Westminster's reputation deep in the gutter but also numbed the reaction from the British electorate to the extent that new scandals have become somewhat normalised. Whilst I find this situation infuriating, I was left sickened to come across some articles reporting that some MPs, each carrying a statutory voting right in the House of Commons, were entertained by and/or sat on the payroll of gambling companies... during the period when parliament was forming revisions to the Gambling Act, aimed at reducing the batting harm through tougher legislation!

The "former chair of the all-party parliamentary group on betting and gaming, was hired by the influential Betting and Gaming Council (BGC) back in October 2020"
The MP was paid £24,000 per annum, the same as average annual UK salary in 2022 (based on ONS data) for working just 10 hours a month. Is it surprising that the unnamed MP "has

spoken in Parliament against making gambling rules too strict"?

inews.co.uk

"28s MPs – 19 Conservative and the rest Labour – have taken almost £225,000 in wages and freebies from the gambling industry since August 2020." During a parliamentary debate concerning revisions to the 2005 gambling act MP Scott Benton "referred to the urgent need to "improve and continue Britain's attractiveness" as a casino destination." Benton "had recently been a guest of the Paddy Power owner, Flutter, at England's match against Germany, and was due to attend the cricket at Lord's the following month, at a cost of £874.80 to the BGC, whose members include major casino companies".

The Guardian

Maybe it's me but it doesn't sit well that our parliamentary system allows MPs, who will give the usual soundbites (on camera) pointing to their concerns about problem gambling, can be paid and/or entertained by the very sector sitting at the heart of the problem? What makes it even more farcical is that some of them have also addressed gambling charity conferences advocating their support in the fight against addiction. Hypocrisy at its worst!

Chapter 10
The Breadwinner's Secret

Having a heightened level of anxiety acts as an almighty barrier to the ability of an addict to transition from someone having every decision made for them by an inner destructive force, dominating every element of their cognitive thinking, to being capable of making independent choices in life. To stand the greatest chance of recovery from addiction, space between an addict and the things that trigger anxious feelings is paramount... in most cases an over-anxious mind will only resort to the tried and tested unhealthy coping mechanisms in search of what is an entirely false sense of security.

But what if one of the anxiety triggers is one that's not only impossible to avoid, its also in the environment where on balance we spend most of our time? That would be work!

If were to ask my wife what she thinks has been the single biggest trigger of compensatory anorexic behaviours during the height of my illness, she'd without doubt say that it was my work.

There's a distinct possibility that some of the opening sentiment in this chapter could be seen as a pre-cursor to a handful of cheap shots being fired at my past/present employers in some kind of narcissistic attempt to distance myself from any personal accountability linked to my now elongated relationship addiction. Setting the record straight from the outset, I'm the first to recognise that **I own** the crippling anxiety I've experienced at work over recent years, a challenge which on the whole sits in the past. Yes, the avoidable chaos at work, normally driven by corporate business politics, has been far from helpful... but only I can take responsibility for the way I've sometimes reacted to the mess it's generated. That said, these challenges, inherent to a varying degree in most corporate enterprises, are more often than not completely needless, but can trigger heightened and sometimes dangerous levels of anxiety in otherwise brilliant day-to-day employees.

Competency based job interviews are becoming increasingly focused on testing the 'resilience' of job applicants... but resilience to what exactly? Coping with a complex and demanding workload, or working in an environment with zero direction, goalposts that constantly move, and leaders who fixate themselves on protecting their own reputation rather than the interests of their employees? I'll let you decide where I stand on this one!

I'm the first to admit that as a rule I've always placed way too much pressure on myself in a bid to illustrate my worth, a 'double edged sword' trait that creates a passion for high standards (the good) but often accompanied by low self-esteem (the bad). This approach to managing through life, first surfaced in my early teens when I developed an innate fear of failure, driving an acute desire for perfection. In days gone by this mindset left me in a constant state of cognitive turmoil with my inner thoughts acting as both aggressor and victim. It took years for me to unearth the likely cause for this irrational approach to life, therapy eventually pointing me back to my childhood as a lad seeking recognition from his dad…although like most of these things, I suspect this won't be the full story.

Anyway, back to the matters at hand. The challenge faced when entering the pressure cooker that is the London Financial Services (FS) sector, with a desire to rise the ranks, can be f*cking tough for anyone carrying a single ounce of self-doubt or all-round mental fragility. If you're technically well equipped to progress to a senior level but equally unfortunate enough to be a self-doubter/anxious person and come from a working-class background, the chances of success aren't impossible, but in my view remain slim.

An ever-increasing focus has emerged in recent years across both insurance and banking sectors to recruit towards creating greater diversity across the workforce. Whilst the opportunity for a butcher's stepson without a university degree to climb to the heady heights of Director isn't impossible, it remains bl**dy tough to achieve. Yep, that would be me, no degree and carrying a noticeable north London working-class twang!

When I first entered the insurance sector, I was the classic 'square peg in a round hole' when it came to my chances of ending up in an Exec role. That said, with a lot of f*cking hard work, I didn't do too bad, landing my first junior FD (Finance Director) role back in 2010. Accompanying this was a constant inner need to justify myself as equally capable as my largely Oxbridge educated peers. This 'need', all of my own making, took its toll on both my mental wellbeing and my family… consistently working ridiculous hours just to prove my value to the business. That said, I don't regret the sacrifices I made to help build a solid start to life for my kids. My sole career regret to date is that I blinked back in 2014, allowing addiction to drag me down a couple of pegs on the career ladder, a situation I've been working hard to rectify since 2019.

I've been with my current employer for a few years now, a big insurance company. It's significantly better than previous organisations I've worked for, largely down to some great people I work with and a boss, who whilst incredibly demanding (and late for every meeting), is as genuine and real as they come. Put it this way, when I decided to 'come out' in early 2021 by publicising my male anorectic status, he didn't batter an eyelid.

Yes, the people in my local business unit make work rewarding from a relationship perspective, but it still shares many of the negative attributes engrained across the FS sector… working stupid hours just to be able to make a difference, wading through treacle like politics, and of course watching your back in case you need to duck the odd machete. The same attributes played their role in my temporary career collapse that followed my dad's passing. My dad's death proved to be the trigger event that pushed me over the edge, but if truth be known, I was already on a path to becoming an addict during the year before he died.

The subject of organisational design and culture fascinates me. This brings me to an old but really interesting article that I recently stumbled across, written by Dr Michael Sinclair, and published by the Financial Times. In the article, Dr Sinclair, a City of London based psychologist unpicked the key elements of the FS sector culture that simultaneously have an adverse impact on employee wellbeing and deny businesses from reaching their full earnings potential.

Dr Sinclair observed the "tremendous" number of bankers and lawyers with work-induced anxiety. "They work at a relentless pace," he says. "The pressure is always on and there is a culture of incessant email communication." But he also believes there is a bigger problem for companies... an intense and highly infectious level of anxiety ... "A company's fear of failure breeds the same fear among its employees creating a company sickness and culture of anxiety,".... "Ironically this backfires, impacting the bottom line."

The point Sinclair makes concerning the impact of a culture founded on fear on the profit potential of a business is 100% bang on the money. As humans we're all born to make mistakes, so a zero-tolerance policy when it comes to f*ck ups does nothing more than breed a culture of conservatism, politics, and cover-ups. Having worked for a couple of businesses falling firmly into this category (not current), I've seen with my own eyes the cottage industry of internal politics and in-fighting created by fear ... all of which served to distract from the primary aim of delivering on behalf of their customers. Allowing employees to make mistakes, and most importantly helping them learn from the experience, is fundamental enabler to create a motivated, happy, and loyal workforce. When a motivated workforce is accompanied by strong leadership and a sound business strategy a business is usually onto a winner!

I'd expect some of my insurance sector peers, especially those working in the London market, to interpret some of my sentiment as an unjustified attack on the industry… the likely response being something along the lines of "if you can't f*cking handle the heat, get the f*ck out of the kitchen". I'm known for my straight-talking approach, so I carry a degree of sympathy for this point of view. If I hadn't been through the sh*t I've dealt with since my mid 30's, I'd have probably given the same response… after all, back then, with the money rolling how could I have seen the underlying damage being caused by my professional life?

In the early post-pandemic period, there was a plethora of LinkedIn posts from people announcing career moves away FS, most citing a desire for more balance and fulfilment in working life. For the masses in the FS sector yet to bring in the big bucks and unable to take the inevitable pay cut that usually comes with a total change in specialism (e.g., moving from Finance to Operations), they can also find it incredibly hard to transfer their existing skills into different industries. Why? Personal experience tells me this challenge isn't usually down to the ability of an individual to perform well in a "same skill/different sector" role. Instead, it's usually driven by a preconception in hiring business that result in concerns about 'cultural fit'. I've been approached by recruitment agencies in the past about some really interesting roles in both retail and manufacturing sectors, only to have my CV dismissed at the first hurdle, purely down to my FS background.

In extreme cases toxic working cultures can prove fatal. Back in 2015, during my final year working at RSA, a large UK based insurer with a history spanning over 300 years, it was subject to a takeover bid from rival Swiss insurer, Zurich. My job at the time saw me pulled into the 'insider' group supporting the executive team over an intense period preparing RSA's response to the bid. The takeover ultimately failed after Zurich's balance sheet was hit by a huge insurance claim (from recollection in China), but a year later Martin Senn, CEO of Zurich Group, committed suicide, with some reports pointing to the failed bid as the catalyst. This came just 3 years after Zurich's Chief Financial Officer, Pierre Wauthier, had also committed suicide.

How could two men, both likely to have built enough personal wealth over their career to make a successful city trader jealous, resort to such drastic action? It was reported by Reuters that in Pierre Wauthier's suicide note he described "becoming demoralised by what he called a new, more aggressive tone at Zurich". Linking this back to the damning points on the FS sector made by Dr Michael Sinclair, could it be that Martin Senn's failure execute the RSA buy-out ultimate proved too much for him in a working culture where failure was deemed as an inconceivable option?

In my darkest days following my father's death, suicide also become a very real option for me. It was clear to everyone I worked closely with that I'd reached crisis point, but did my employer do the right thing by insisting that I take time out or recommend I take an occupational health assessment? If they had of, it would make this section pretty pointless! After two weeks compassionate leave just after dad died I was back in the pressure cooker (the office), fueled by the knowledge that any more time out would leave me having to work ridiculous hours just to catch up with my work. My gradual path to self-destruction was visible to all, losing weight, carrying a volatile mood, and I'd even started smoking again having quit 10 years earlier. Yes, I should have asked my GP to sign me off work, but the reality was that I'd been left zero cognitive reasoning ability and needed my employer to tell me to go home and take an extended break.

With both my health and performance at work deteriorating, I managed to last just over a year before signing a mutual agreement to terminate my employment with RSA, leaving with a monetary package... i.e, I got a pay-out and I suspect that most importantly for them, my employer got a 'problem' off their books! At the time, with my state of mind in tatters, what presented as a catastrophic career failure in a sector based on reputation, also presented itself a perfect reason to finally end my life. I thought about it long and hard but it's clear that I didn't. I want to say that it was the love of my wife, kids, mum, and stepdad that stopped me, but the fact is my family never actually factored into my thinking. What actually stopped me was my inability to find a scenario that ticked both of my essential suicide boxes... the endgame would be both instantaneous and it could never be at the expense of a traumatic experience on the part of an innocent third party or family member. You try and think of a scenario that ticks both boxes.

So, after all my moaning about the industry sector that to this day helps us pay the mortgage, why the hell haven't I jumped ship in search of greater fulfilment in my professional life? To start with and despite being far from perfect, the business I work for is better than other companies I've worked for in the past, largely down to a handful of great people. Then there's the age old saying "the grass isn't always greener...".

Does it make me a complete hypocrite, doing a full 180 degree turn from some of the sentiment in this chapter, suggesting the FS sector could remain career home until I finally retire? Well, not quite when you consider the following:

The Family Breadwinner

It's common that a single member of the family unit earns a disproportionate amount of the household income. This imbalance is often a conscious decision made by a couple, just as my wife and I did when our kids were younger. My wife, also a qualified accountant …I've heard every wise crack known to man about how exciting our marriage must be!... could easily have gone on to build a great career for herself, but circumstances at home meant one of us had to make a sacrifice. We needed parental presence in the family home to support our son's early stages of development, after he was diagnosed with speech and language delays. If we hadn't had made the decision to cut my wife's working days, I've no doubt we'd never have seen the remarkable progress in his development we've witnessed over the years, leaving him struggling academically and carrying some really challenging behaviours.

It's all well and good if you're the family breadwinner working in a job you love, but let's be honest, the number of us sat in this category will undoubtably be disproportionately low. This leaves the rest of us working in a job or industry sector until we have that lightbulb moment, often brought on by the new perspective on life we get in our 40's, finally seeing a lack of professional fulfilment. By this time, with age against us and an over reliance on a need to earn to maintain a family lifestyle, it's often impossible to take a different career path, even if this could be beneficial for our own wellbeing.

Like many others in my situation, who I'd say are disproportionately men, I'm likely to be tied to both career and industry, bound by a need to earn for my family rather than a choice to spend 50-60 hours of my week wedded to them. Whilst not as extreme in my case, for others, it can feel like a prison sentence, incarcerated until they reach the point of retirement. I often wonder whether there's a link between this common problem and the alarming number of suicides we see in men in their 40's?

I know my wife and I made the right decision in creating an imbalance in our respective earning potential. Had we not made that decision, both our kids would never have benefited from the development they've had, largely down to her efforts. I've lost count of the number of times she's told me to find a job earning half as much, but one I would enjoy. Whilst the thought is appealing, practical thinking tells me that it would never work. The only real option would be for me to it alone in something totally different, but this is well beyond my family risk appetite. Frustrating as it may be, I'm a stereotypical guy with DNA that tells me to grit my teeth and crack on provide the best for the loved ones who surround. It doesn't make it right, but it is what it is!

An Influence for Change

Remaining wedded to a sector carrying cultural traits that 'resilience' struggles to ignore actually gives me a weird sense of purpose… to continue challenging some of the deep-rooted issues in an effort to open up a few Boardroom eyes to the opportunity brought by change. An old saying springs to mind, one that my grandad often used … the chance of me being able to open up a discussion about change is likely to be greater if I remain an industry insider. Where's the "age old saying"?... those famous words first used by President Lyndon Johnston back in 1971… "Better to have your enemies inside the tent pi**ing out, than outside the tent pi**ing in". If I can talk and write openly about my personal experience at the hands of needless corporate cultural challenges in my chosen career sector, I live in hope that it will resonate in others, possibly a couple sitting at the top who may be willing to consider gambling on a different way of working…. There's knout wrong with hope, even if it is proved to be delusional!

<u>Takeaways</u>

If you've arrived at this point in the chapter thinking this guy is both delusional and taking a big risk with some potentially career limiting sentiment, these are conclusions I've also toyed with. But you'd be way off the mark when it comes to the intent behind the sentiment. My primary aim in bringing some well-known but largely ignored issues to the surface is to help open up a mindset that that a different approach could be beneficial to all... customers, shareholders, employees... and Directors! I've had no real choice but to single out Financial Services, the only sector I'm semi-qualified to write about after years of first-hand experience... an industry I know is far from alone in carrying engrained elements of cultural toxicity, but the one I know best!

The harsh reality is, regardless of industry sector, businesses carrying toxic cultural traits would benefit from taking a long look at themselves in the mirror! The response from corporate employers over recent years to the problem of work-based anxiety has largely been fragmented and often lacking in purpose. From my perspective it's usually limited to virtue signalling internal comms about the importance of employee well-being, with limited to no action to evidence the sentiment. This is normally accompanied by the provision of self-help advice and tools (i.e., enabling employees to **cope with** fundamental business issues rather **actually address** them). Laying on fruit or setting up a pool table for employees in the office, providing online mental health seminars or free access to digital wellbeing apps prompting you to breathe deeply or go for a walk are all helpful, but in my mind, nothing more than 'Wellbeing Washing' strategies... they fail to tackle the root causes of poor employee well-being. In some cases, I'd go as far as saying that corporate Wellbeing strategies actually point solely at the individual as the cause of the challenges they face in a work setting.

Papering over the cracks with reactive assistance for employees who in a good environment are more than capable of excelling in their job, but feel like sh*t, struggling to cope with workload and the strain of Westminster style internal politics, is both expensive and simply not the answer. Unlocking the door to improved mental health in the workplace, better productivity, and service to customers, all of which drive improved profitability, can only happen with root and branch cultural change, starting right at the top in the boardroom.

If my industry sector decides to 'cancel' me for publicly calling out some of the fundamental challenges that impact thousands of its employees, I guess I'll just have to suck it up and face the consequences. For me, it's more important that I stand by the principle that speaking openly carries the greatest chance of someone out there actually listening!

A FORNIGHT 'FUNCTIONING' WITH ADDICTION

Blah Blah, F*cking Blah!

WEEK 1

CHAPTER 11
The Team Lunch

Today presented me with a situation that in the ordinary day-to-day life of the sane among us would be a mere run of the mill event. In my case it creates a whirlwind of wholly irrational thinking that ends up sending me close to rails. I'd known today has been coming since last month, but over recent years I've become used ignoring the opportunity provided by advanced warning to prepare the mind for dealing with a perceived threat. Following the usual script, yet again I fail to stem the flow of inner tension that's built up in small increments to a near uncontrollable level over the last couple of weeks. In the not too distant days gone by I'd have been quick to execute an exit strategy with complete military precision simply to avoid a perfectly normal situation the majority of people would look forward to. I'd select one of the many convoluted excuses from the vast back catalogue I've worked hard to build over the years. Why think in this way? It comes down to a completely false mental perception that comes a genuine feeling that my very existence is under genuine threat.

Back in 2019, carrying an unspoken but clearly tarnished reputation in my industry sector (simply for showing human vulnerability) I finally landed a job following 8 months of applications, joining a recognisable multi-national insurance business to head up the finance team of one of its smaller subsidiary businesses. This team and I would end up going through a pretty seismic, but ultimately successful period of both functional and broader business change.

A couple of months after joining the business I recall thinking "what the hell have you signed up for here?". Morale across my team was at rock bottom, they no sense of empowerment, and there was a visible daily fire fight just to keep their heads above water. It was clear to all including the guys on the ground that a big 'fix it' job was needed. At the time they were blissfully unaware of the stage 2 plan… to lift and drop what was a vastly different and in many ways a uniquely complex business into its parent company (the whole shebang - people, IT systems, operational processes etc.). Sound like a load of corporate bullsh*t rather than plain English? Translated: we had some pretty big sh*t to deliver starting from a pretty f*cking poor position. In even simpler terms (nearer to my level), akin to when Leicester City won the Premier League back in 2016, just two years after being promoted from the Championship.

The team were based in an old office in Eastbourne. It was like a scene out of the early 90's… outdated computers and office furniture similar to the sort of cr*p once sold by MFI. Eastbourne, seaside town in southern England, was far from head office, a place best known for being a mecca for the "mature" generation (in 2013, at 70, it had the highest average resident age in England). The town is lightyears away from the type of location you'd expect to find a division of multi-national business and unlike London, where I'd spent most of my working life, experience delivering complex business change programmes was pretty thin on the ground. With an 'evergreen' pool of talent, I set upon working with the team I'd inherited to manage through the complexity we'd been tasked to deliver. From there, I'd be wholly understated in saying that they've surpassed every expectation I first had, showing an innate willingness and ability to deliver.

In a little under two weeks, with the exception of one guy who will remain reporting into me (top bloke with a heart of gold), the entire team I inherited back in 2019 who travelled with me through such a tough but ultimately brilliant journey will transition into the 'mothership' finance function. Largely down to natural staff attrition rather than forced redundancies, they are now half the in size they once were, but the guys remaining them having built a solid reputation across the wider parts of the business. Having been on the journey with them, I've seen individuals grow in stature both professionally and personally. Today was my chance to say a massive "thank you" to them by taking them out for a thoroughly well-deserved celebratory team lunch.

Sound like an occasion for anyone sat in the saine category to look forward? Of course, it bl**dy does! But as things stand my binary 'addict' thinking, which has become so entrenched from years living with anorexia, wouldn't even give me a free pass on this important occasion. It couldn't allow me to see past the fact that I'll be eating earlier than normal and won't have full control over what I eat. In this type of scenario, the rational side of my brain, now weakened to the point where it sometimes barely registers a voice, stands little to no chance of stopping my thinking from going into disarray. The reaction then takes then takes its usual course, following the same old f*cking script I've lived each and every day since 2014... "Have we booked a restaurant with low calorie options?... must check the online menu... any decent excuses I can come up with to avoid going?". Blah, blah, f*cking blah!

Any half decent leader will know that a combination of presence and presenting as your true self in the workplace can perform wonders when it comes to getting the best out of the people who work for you. Recognising this led to the usual deep and vert dark addiction led guilt for even considering the option to avoid the chance to celebrate with a team of people who worked incredibly hard for me.

Thankfully, after what can only be described as a childlike discussion with my wife... "should I allow myself to go?" (I've lost count of the number of times she's helped in this type of situation) ... I was given some rational words of advice that enabled me to muster the necessary strength to throw myself in the deep end and go. During the lunch I feel massively on edge as some of the team tuck into their massive gastro burgers deep filled homemade pies, with me settling for my middle eastern grilled chicken kebabs with wild rice and a raita dip. I just hope the team didn't notice the tension through the somewhat falsified smile on my face.

I genuinely enjoyed the chance to say a massive thank you and celebrate my team's achievements over a well-deserved lunch, but the usual post-mortem of this type of very common situation always feels like swallowing a bitter pill for me. Still, I take comfort in knowledge I ended up doing the right thing for them, and in a strange way, myself. The only way I can move out of what is a never-ending cycle of addiction led thoughts and behaviours is to challenge the underlying 'musts' / 'must nots' that come with my illness. Yes, it felt f*cking uncomfortable, but the experience gave me one of those rare opportunities to raise a firm middle finger right in the face of anorexia nervosa.

CHAPTER 12
The Anorectic Encounter

"If the kindest soles were rewarded with longest lives, dogs would outlive us all"

Ricky Gervais

The end of a hectic working day is normally marked with a walk, just me and the dog, normally accompanied by a thought provoking/comical podcast. Cooper, my 3-year-old 'salt and pepper' miniature schnauzer, is everyone's friend, but he's my absolute best mate… which does say a great deal for my social life! Carrying the usual terrier traits, he f*cking hates the postman, steals anything when an opportunity presents (especially my socks), is an all-round smart cookie, and follows me absolutely everywhere. But the thing that really makes him stand out is his innate ability to smell the scent of a low mood from a mile away, knowing exactly when to interrupt a negative thought process with affection.

We all know that pets can be both costly and act as a huge tie on family life. But for those suffering with acute or simply prone to bouts of anxiety/depression, the company of a K9 can provide an instant and highly effective stabiliser that's miles better by any big pharma anti-depressant. The parallels between dog ownership and day-to-day parenting can be stark, the rewards usually contingent on the right upbringing. But, unlike the point when our kids enter their teenage years, the love from a dog is always genuine, never dwindles and comes without a single string or pound sign attached. Us humanoids could and should learn a lot from these amazing animals when it comes to the way we go about daily life!

Out with Cooper this evening, the sun dipping below the distant Surrey hills, I bump into a lady walking her spaniel. The dogs make their usual acquaintances, a quick sniff of the rear end followed by a mutual inspection of the 'crown jewels'. I recognise the lady, I'd say in her late 50's, as a runner I'd encountered in days gone by whilst pounding the streets every morning at a time when the sane among us are firmly tucked up in bed with 2-3 hours to go until the dreaded alarm chimes.

This was the first time I'd bumped into her at walking pace, providing a chance to exchange the usual niceties rather than the standard runner's salute or nod we'd exchanged in the past. I mention in passing that I remember her from my days out running at 'early doors' and ask if she was still hitting the pavements. She told me that running remained very much part of her weekly routine, but I was left lost for words by her very open and totally unprompted admission that her routine had strayed into addiction that led to her own encounter with an eating disorder. Her remarkable openness with me (a complete stranger) about very personal level of vulnerableness made it a completely safe environment for me to talk about my own encounter with the anorectic devil.

As we got talking and sharing stories, she opened up about the time when it finally hit home that exercise had transitioned from a once healthy pastime to a body and mind destroying routine. She'd travelled to Bangkok with her husband and children, but spent the entire fortnight compelled by no one but herself to run a minimum 10k distance on the hotel treadmill before she'd 'allow' herself (and her family) to start each day of the holiday.

Hearing her account of a trip to South-East Asia being marred by a distraction to addiction led "musts" stirs up memories of my time in Vietnam back in 2016. Back then I was at the height of the addiction cycle, anorexia holding a tight and very short leash around my neck which left my all-round state of health at rock bottom. With things so bad I mutually agreed an incentivised contract termination with my employer (covered in chapter 10). Desperately needing to distance myself from a professional setting that only served to fuel my illness, the plan was to take a 3-month sabbatical to focus on climbing out of the ditch I'd dug for myself. Like so many other false promises that come with addiction the reality turned out to be the complete opposite of the plan. During my break, I somehow managed to persuade my wife that some time away in unfamiliar surroundings would give me the distance I needed from my domestic life to work things through in my head. I'm not someone to do things by halves so after receiving the green light from a very understanding wife I flew out to Vietnam with nothing but a rucksack and train tickets, embarking on a solo adventure that would see me travel the 1500km from Hanoi in the north to Saigon (Ho Chi Minh City) via public transport.

After a near 22-hour sleep deprived journey to Hanoi I arrived at the £18 a night Win Hotel feeling absolutely shattered. At this point a balanced individual would hit the sack for few hours to recharge their thoroughly drained batteries… but not me! What did I do? I got my running kit on, laced up my Asics and headed out for a 10k run lapping Hoan Kiem Lake in the centre of Hanoi. It was mid-afternoon, the temperature around

35 degrees and air dense as the oxygen fought for space with the exhaust fumes from the thousands of motorbikes and tuc tucs circling the lake… you could literally chew on it! But despite the sleep deprivation and appalling running conditions I HAD to get my fix! The run ended with me arriving back at the hotel only to collapse on my bed, falling into a deep sleep.

I stayed in Hanoi for 3 days before taking a coach alongside other back packers to Ha Long Bay. The morning of my departure still holds firm in my mind as I headed down to the hotel lobby for an early morning run to find half of the staff sleeping on the tiled reception floor. The fright I gave them is now laughable as my 6' 3" pastie white skeleton of a frame interrupted their sleep at 5:30am, politely asking (in a very British way) if the hotel door could be unlocked to allow me to head out once again into the Hanoi smog.

My Vietnam adventure was meant to reconnect my mind to the world around me. Slumming it on less than desirable (but fun) public transport all the way from Hanoi down to Ho Chi Minh City (Via Ha Long Bay, Nha Trang and Hoi An) was nothing short of a massive eye opener, leaving me with memories that I'll never let go of. Whilst I did feel a degree of much needed disconnect from the daily grind back in the UK, exploring what is an amazing country steeped in rich history, my adventure came with firm strings attached to my eating disorder.... I 'went on tour' but despite the absence of a passport, it didn't stop anorexia from smuggling itself onto the plane with me.

Hoan Kiem lake, Hanoi (2016)

Look at the f*cking state I was in!

With both dogs and dog walkers having said their goodbyes after 20mins of sniffing and talking, I spend the rest of Cooper's walk pondering over just how widespread the situation I've been in over recent years could actually be... seemingly 'normal' people to the naked eye going about their daily business whilst hiding an existence chained under lock and key to a series of crippling addiction fueled "musts" and "must nots".

WEEK 2

CHAPTER 13
Kings

I a regular at Kings (my local leisure centre) to such an extent that I'm on first name terms with all the lifeguards and the receptionists have already checked me in for a swim before I've had a chance to say "good morning" to them. The staff must think I'm either insane (which wouldn't be far off the truth) or the centre is my place of worship!

A few weeks back the centre announced it would be shutting the pool for a week to allow for essential pool maintenance… hardly headline grabbing news to the reader, but for me it came with a feeling similar to thinking I'd won the lottery only to realise that I forgot to buy the ticket! Ever since I saw the announcement anorexia has been counting down the days, hours, and seconds to closure. In the final week I felt like I was in a scene from one of those god-awful 1990's Hollywood action films… tension building (accompanied by cr*p 'Beverley Hills Cop' style backing track) as the final seconds pass in the countdown to detonation… only for Keanu Reeves (other sh*t actors are available!) to appear from nowhere to randomly stumble across and defuse the device with seconds left, preventing a school full to the brim with perfect Hollywood children (that simply don't exist in real life) from being blown to smithereens!

These days I'm no longer compelled to exercise to the extreme levels that once dominated daily life. But I still need a 30-40min cardio 'fix' at least six times a week, the intent now switched from the destruction of targeted weight loss to a strategy I use to keep my inner demons at bay. It's been over a year since I laced up my Asics and headed out for a run. Swimming is now my sole cardio coping mechanism. A couple of years ago I'd have sniggered at the sort of guys who see any appeal in the continuous back and forth down a lane of cold chlorinated water in skin-tight shorts. Now, I'm a full convert, loving that buzz from that initial submersion that delivers a head-to-toe temperature shock and the constant flow of water into my ears serving to distract my mind from the usual cycle of addiction inspired compulsive thoughts.

Swimming provides a level of stress relief and all-round mental stimulation that goes way beyond anything I ever got from crossing the tape at the end of a marathon. This alone leaves me sh*tting my pants at the thought of having to manage for a whole week without my go-to form of therapy. Ironically, possibly presenting a glimmer of hope that my mindset is starting to 'normalise', I actually find a small level of comfort in the knowledge that the challenge I face actually provides me with an opportunity to test my engrained way of thinking ... forcing me to deal with the discomfort from what I know will feel similar to my experience of withdrawal from Pregabalin.

One thing that experience has shown is that I now face a heightened risk that my still dominate eating disorder voice will demand that I find alternative ways to burn a minimum calorific target just to be allowed to follow my normal eating pattern (well, 'normal' for me)... the same type of reaction you'd expect from alcoholic when their local drinking hole unexpectedly closes... Whilst they might commit to a week of sobriety the reality is they won't wait for the pub to re-open to get their next pint! The daily life of an addict is dominated by an inner voice that promises to change tomorrow but when tomorrow finally arrives the intended change always shifts out to the next day. With this in mind, I know that I'm facing into a f*cking tough few days. I MUST celebrate any learnings I take from the experience that could present a marginal gain towards recovery.

Monday: Day 3

Thankfully, day 1 and 2 of 'shutdown' fall on the weekend,

always a busy for us with the kid's sport, sleepovers and the usual in and outside chores… all helping to distract the mind.

Monday arrives within the blink of an eye and it's back to work, making it a tough day without the stress relief from my usual short but long-lasting cardio burst. Three days without a fix leaves my insides approaching boiling point, compounded by an idiotic decision to work in isolation at home rather than benefit from the company of others in the office.

The pandemic has made hybrid working the norm across many industry sectors, the balance of power between employer and employee now shifted towards the later. This is evidenced by the candidate led recruitment market (in 2022) where hybrid working has become an expectation versus a traditionally by-exception arrangement. Yes, hybrid working does provide priceless flexibility for a busy family unit, but heavily weighted working from home patterns come with big downsides for both employer and employee.

I see working life as being like a second marriage. I my opinion when the relationship converts to a long distance one driven by disproportionate levels of home working, the overall health and longevity of the marriage are both put at risk. There is no way that either employees can be as productive, or businesses can benefit from essential in-person working relationships if everyone is stuck at home using Skype or Teams as their only channel of communication. Added to this and bringing it back to the subject matter at hand, the highly secretive behaviours associated with addiction can make home working the perfect breeding ground for an addiction to manifest and flourish. Put simply, it's far easier for an addict to adhere to their inner demands when they're 'out of sight, out of mind'.

Tuesday: Day 4

By now I'm climbing the walls. I f*cking need to exercise if I'm to stop my brain from imploding! Yes, a 45-minute walk at lunchtime with Cooper is always a pleasure, seeing him enjoy the temporary freedom, but I feel like a caged animal fully prepared to attack as soon as the door opens. The inner tension is indescribable!

After a full-on day working at home, sat in back-to-back Teams meetings exchanging dignified pleasantries with colleagues, resolving complex challenges, and of course, keeping my seniors satisfied that I'm on top of everything, I finish the day utterly drained. Living with a double identity (professional addict and professional accountant), constantly having to mask any trace of my addiction to the professional world, is utterly exhausting.

It gets to 6pm and having started my day at 7:30am, I throw in the towel and drive 10 miles to the nearest open leisure centre for a swim. I enter the Olympic sized pool, immersing myself in the cooler than usual water and once again I feel. After smashing out 2km it's back home to deal with the usual backlog of emails built up over the course of the day whilst I've been sat in a plethora of Teams meetings.

Wednesday: Day 5

Yesterday evening's endorphin fix wore off pretty fast as I wake up in the morning with an immediate thirst for another high. Somehow, I manage to stay strong, avoiding the temptation to repeat last night's 20-mile round trip for another swim, but it's f*cking hard! My mind constantly interrupts me throughout the day with exercise related thoughts, doing its upmost to distract me from the work deadlines I've committed to hit.

The evening brings some light relief delivered by a football training session my junior team and a sunset walk with my trusty Schnauzer sidekick.

Thursday: Day 6

For anyone who's never witnessed or experienced workings of anorexia nervosa, the thought of only one workout in five days will be trivial matter, and for some, one too many. For me and other likeminded anorectics, this type of situation is far from trivial, leaving us in a constant battle our own minds. That said, the last 5 days have been a mini landmark moment in my struggle beat this illness… I actually had a rare moment this morning, feeling a small sense of pride in myself… it didn't last long but presented a small glimmer of hope!

I spend the day in the office today, mostly sat in meetings, but with other human beings sat in the same room. I leave the office around 7pm after a busy day but one I've enjoyed owing to the social interaction I've had. As soon as my car kicks into life my mind immediately switches direction, becoming polarised on one thing… exercise! My thinking goes into overdrive, scenario planning multiple strategies to satisfy what's becoming an uncontrollable urge. The meticulous planning my brain goes through is akin to a military General simulating a plan to attack enemy held territory. The energy consumed going through this process, one I've been through on countless occasions over recent years, is exhausting!

I arrive home, decision made (well, made for me) … I'm going for a run! I spent over ten years running, initially to get fit, then using it as a means to socialise, and finally, enjoying the competition presented by the southeast race calendar. All good and beneficial to every aspect of my health until the balance tipped and it became the primary channel to feed an addiction! Having slipped back into old bad habits over the multitude of pandemic lockdowns I managed to 'give up' over a year ago, switching to the pool… but with no other option available to me right here, right now, I lace up and head out.

It's a bright spring evening, 15 degrees with a light cooling breeze…"perfect conditions" I tell myself. The inner voice would say anything to justify this is as a sensible decision despite the obvious risk of relapse into old health destroying behaviours.

I arrive home from work, change into my kit and head out, dropping my daughter at her gymnastics session before heading to the local station carpark marking the midway point of the Worth Way... once a coastal railway track, now a bridleway and my old stomping ground (for running). The route is planned; 2 ¼ miles along to Crawley Down pond and back. The planned 4 ½ mile ends up being extended by a mile as the highly persuasive voice suggests that it'd be "just like old times" if I take a detour via a field I'd always enjoyed running through.

Arriving back at the car, I look and feel no different to when I crossed the finish line back in my marathon days. Admittedly I am thirteen years older than when I finished my first ever marathon. At the same time science would suggest that age is not the reason why 5 ½ miles left me feeling utterly f*cked. The reality is that despite my recovery to a status of functioning anorectic, I remain a stone lighter of muscle mass than back then. Yes, the NHS tells me that my BMI is "healthy", but it's far from sufficient to give me the stamina and speed I once had.

Friday: Day 7

At last, the final day of 'shutdown' arrives... thank f*ck for that! I wake up, legs feeling like led weights, leaving me struggling to lift them out of bed unaided. As any amateur long-distance runner knows, heading down a set of stairs is the hardest thing the day after running a marathon (ironically, going up is okay). If you're ever in the city the morning after the London Marathon, look out for the commuters heading to work, clasping onto the handrail for dear life as make their way down the steps to the tube... it's hilarious! I feel just like one of those casualties, hamstrings tied in knots as I carefully make my way down to the kitchen for a pre-school run coffee... broken, having run less than a quarter of the 26.2 mile marathon distance last night!

Exercise limited to two days out of six. Can I make it two out of seven? Hell no! Despite the concentration of lactic acid in my legs building hour by hour, I force myself to the gym in the evening for a workout. I hate the gym… cardio machines providing the opportunity to move without actually going anywhere, leaving me routed to the spot on the treadmill with no entertainment other than the weightlifters admiring the beauty of their body as they execute the next bicep curl with precision. Forcing myself to go to the gym in a conscious effort to burn calories when I'm hardly moving with ease does end up casting a small shadow over what has otherwise been a groundbreaking week for me. I've successfully restricted my exercise without the sky falling in!

ADDICTION RECOVERY THEORY

&

THE PERSONALISED PLAN

CHAPTER 14
Recovery Theory & Planning

I've spent 7 long years, initially off the rails, followed by a gradual transition to a functioning state, but continue to live in a rigid daily cycle of addiction that I must find a way to sever. If not for the sake of my own health, then for the sake of my wife's sanity, now is the time for me to cut the remaining ties to anorexia that continue to make each and every sunrise the start of yet another Groundhog Day. My illness has not only restricted all of our lives for years, the stagnation over the last few has been frustrating for all... and it's also left everyone f*cking bored of the 'same sh*t, different day' routine!

There have been too many attempts to divorce myself from anorexia using a mix of the 'stop all exercise / eat like a horse' recovery programmes prescribed by healthcare professionals, and as you'd expect, a plethora of self-help programmes. Being someone who's wholly tuned into my faults I recognise that this failure is in part down to an innate stubbornness to solve problems my way! Failure aside, now feels like the right time to try something new by testing an approach I've pondered over for some time...the 1% principle! I'm yet to stumble across the concept in the world of 'self-help', but it's one that I've used with a degree of success in my professional life having been hooked by the success it's had in enhancing performance in the world of professional sport.

This untried concept in the world of addiction recovery (I think!) is founded on the application of 'marginal gains' theory... which I'm now betting big on to give me the best chance of finally breaking free from the constraints that continue to dominate my life.

Marginal Gains Theory

Borne out of 'Kaizen', Japanese for "continuous improvement", marginal gains theory was a concept successfully applied by the Japanese in their effort to rebuild after the second world war that left both the country's morale and infrastructure in tatters. The underpinning ethos of marginal gains theory is the concept that small and most importantly, continuous improvements, generate a compound effect, turning tiny increments into 'big step' performance change. A well-publicised more recent application of this theory sits with the spectacular results achieved by the British Cycling in the 2012 London Olympics, having transformed from a poorly performing team to world beaters under the leadership of Sir Dave Brailsford.

Brailsford transformed the British Cycling team from mediocrity to top of the pack using the concept of continuous small but wide-reaching changes... improvements to **every** part of the bike design and athlete nutrition/fitness. He adopted a deep-rooted scientific approach identifying and making microscopic improvements across the whole of the British cycling operation that stretched as far as the pillows the athletes slept on.

Overkill? Possibly, but Brailsford's obsessive search for improvements no matter how small ended up paying off big time. Team Sky won the Tour de France within three years, two years ahead of target, Bradley Wiggins became the first British cyclist to win the same event, and the British Olympic team won a haul gold medals under his tenure… from a starting medal tally of just a single British gold in the previous 70 years. Remarkable!

The beauty sat at the very heart of marginal gains theory is its simplicity, which probably explains why a shoddy comprehensive school educated guy like me has leaned on it for years in his working life. I often refer to the concept at work to such an extent that I can now see members of my team desperately trying to avoid the temptation to roll their eyes when yet again, I utter the words "consistent small steps in the right direction"... I swear it must sometimes feel for them like working for Uncle Albert ("during the war....")! Anyway, back to the point at hand... if putting this theory into practice has served me well in my professional life, why the f*ck haven't I used it to help address the biggest challenge I've faced in my personal life?

I've read countless 'self-help' books and seen numerous psychologists over the years, all singing from the same addiction recovery hymn sheet... abstinence as the only answer, supported by a prescription medication and thought re-engineering techniques like CBT. That may be the case for drug, alcohol and possibly gambling related addiction, but is it really the only approach to tackle all forms of addiction?

The issue with the 'abstinence is the only way' approach is that it fails to take any account of the bigger picture. When you're the primary breadwinner (as I am) in a job/industry sector where the difference between success and failure is based on building and maintaining a strong reputation of successful delivery, the harsh reality is that you can't just stop everything and go 'cold turkey' for a few weeks/months and then expect everything to return to normal in your professional life. Life simply doesn't work that way! Abstinence may well be the quickest route to an addiction free life, but it fails to consider the practicality of making huge, overnight changes to a malfunctioning lifestyle at the risk of destroying a family's financial stability.

I strongly suspect that I've created a perception that patience is not one of my strongest points. This is going to have to change as I enter my next (and hopefully final) stage of recovery. If I revert to type and dive in too quickly, I know I'll freak out, which will only result in landing on the head of a snake, sending me right back to square one on the game board. I need to get comfortable with I'm only seeking to make small gains over time, no matter how small!

The Recovery Plan

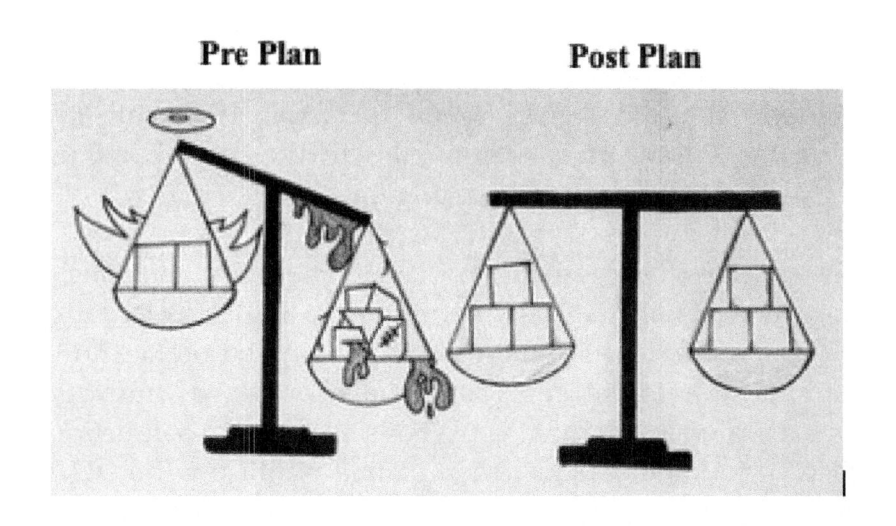

Pre Plan   **Post Plan**

Illustrated by: *My Daughter*

It's dam easy when mentally unwell to convince yourself that you're sh*t at absolutely everything, mustering little to no inner strength to look at things through a more rational lens. Putting yourself down becomes a daily / hourly mantra when you're cognitively weak. It's easy to kick someone when they're already on the floor, which may explain why the brain does just that to its host when feeling in a low state of mind. It takes time, a lot of sole searching and courage when you're feeling anxious/depressed to see through the imperfections and faults that come with our very human existence to identify the individual strengths we **all** carry.

Over the years I've been the butt of many a light-hearted joke at work about my sometimes overzealous eye for detail… if it provides some ammunition for well-mannered banter pointed in my direction, go ahead, take your best a shot! Whether it's an OCD trait or simply an accountant's 'spike strength' (a little more corporate 'bullsh*t bingo') I know that I'll be relying on this to develop the 'small steps' recovery plan I need to target a weakness in the wall that continues to divide my mind between my eating disorder and free thinking. My concern is that my distinct lack of patience will see me revert to type, charging into big changes that will leave me staring down the barrel of failure from 'too much, too soon'. I must stay calm (easier said than done) and remain aligned to the principle of 'small steps', hoping this will see me take down the dividing wall in my mind that is separating sanity from addiction.

I'm a chartered accountant, not a psychologist, meaning my plan of attack will naturally come with a high risk of failure. But hey, it's been well thought through, focused on tackling the remaining day-to-day life constraints presented my eating disorder (refer to Chapter 4: "What's life like as a functioning addict?"). A solid plan accompanied with my determined mindset, which my wife would probably describe as sheer stubbornness, should improve my chance of finally breaking the cycle of addiction that I remain chained to. So, here's my approach to build a recovery plan which I've laid out in 6 simple steps:

Step 1

Identify the addiction led "musts" and "must nots" that dominate your daily existence.

Back in Chapter 3 (Life as a 'Functioning Addict') I brought to life what it's like to live with the constraints associated with the "musts" that usually come hand in hand with addiction... the thoughts and actions that often dominate every hour of an addict's waking day, all linked to a single objective ... to maintain a feeling of being in control which avoids the inevitable barrage of fear fueled anxiety that arrives when the pattern of addiction is threatened.

In my late father's case, a man who sadly spent his final years living as a fully blown alcoholic, it was clear that his first glass of white wine (always with ice) had to enter the bloodstream by absolutely **no later** than 11am. Except from the point that his health deteriorated to such an extent that cancer finally landed him in hospital, I never actually witnessed this personalised "must' of his ever be tested… but can say with a degree of certainty that had this "must" been tested before he fell ill, it would most likely have triggered a mini meltdown. The same situation is faced by anyone living with extreme OCD living life controlled by a constant cycle of repetitive checks and balances that manifest in ritual like methods, cycles, counts… in fact anything that compels them to create those feelings of being safe and in control. The strange behaviours that accompany a condition like OCD (from a 'sane' observer's perspective) are often trivialised or seen as a laughing matter. But the reality is this condition can be just as destructive when it comes to the impact on both physical and mental wellbeing as any other form of addiction.

However ridiculous the "musts" may manifest, someone whose trapped will always comply with them in order to maintain what in truth is an entirely false perception of control.

All you need to do to complete step 1 is to get those "musts" down on paper…. all of them!

Step 2

Separate the "musts" into <u>Primary</u> and <u>Secondary</u> categories.

Primary "musts" are those that cause the deepest, darkest level of discomfort if presented with circumstances that threaten one's ability to conform… i.e., the behaviours that cause the greatest level of mental and often physical harm. An alcoholic's primary need is to maintain/increase the volume of alcohol in the bloodstream. For people with an acute case of anorexia (where I once found myself) they "must" restrict and maintain their net energy consumption at a level below what their body requires to maintain weight. In both cases the associated actions of the addict carry significant consequences for their physical health.

Secondary "musts" are normally interrelated with the primary, but whilst they cause harm, the damage is normally more circumstantial. Using me as a case in point, I "must not" eat breakfast before 11am. The concept of having a late breakfast doesn't actually cause any harm if it comes from an independent decision (i.e., not a hard rule). But in my case, it is a rule, interconnected with the safety I've learnt to feel from the hunger that comes with a restricted energy consumption. See the connection?

When primary and secondary "musts" are combined, maximum harm becomes reality as both body and cognitive autonomy moves from a state of independence to complete fixation on adhering to the demands of the underlying illness.

I fully admit, the whole thing is totally nonsensical and entirely f*cked up, but it's the reality for a growing number of people and my way of articulating the workings of an addiction.

To complete step 2 all you need to do is separate your list (from step 1) into the two categories.

Step 3

Separate your Primary "musts" into two component parts:

Frequency: How often "must" I do it (e.g., how often I must exercise)

Severity: The extent to which I "must" do it? (e.g., how long must I exercise for)

I'd recommend using first person wording when completing this step, with the "I must" helping to add significant weight to the statement.

Focusing **solely** on your primary "musts" now becomes the priority. Why? Put simply, this focuses energy on tackling the behaviours that cause the greatest amount of self-harm.
The foundation of marginal gains theory is small steps in the right direction, the logic being that a couple of shuffles forward will turn into a few steps, then big strides. This provides the momentum needed to challenge the fear/self-doubt that stops someone from making changes to their current way of life. The theory here is the euphoria created from a sense of achievement ends up building inner strength, allowing someone to push harder (the snowball effect).

Step 4

Select the Primary "must" component that would be marginally less painful to challenge? (i.e., how often or the extent to which you must comply).

The very thought of challenging the elements of daily life we use to feel safety, which deep down we know is an entirely false interpretation, usually sparks a fight or flight response. Having spent years in the clasp of anorexia I'm fully tuned into my body's signature response to such a threat. It presents as a sudden muscular freeze lasting no more than a couple of seconds which is swiftly followed by a lightning bolt of cold running through my core accompanied by a pounding heart… to the extent it feels like it could fracture my sternum. If the thought of change leads to similar feelings of panic, I'd advise taking a moment to calm the mind. It's not you operating with an independent mind… it's the threat it presents to the entirely false sense of comfort that your habits lead you to believe!

When the mind settles to a more balanced state, the next step is to be honest with yourself in addressing the question at hand in step 4. For instance, if you've got an unhealthy relationship with alcohol, what would feel more do-able'? Do you start breaking the cycle by having a single alcohol-free day each week or cut your daily consumption by a single unit?

I've purposefully left the door open to different approaches, knowing everyone's mind works differently, something which of course makes each and every one of us unique. In my case the overwhelming primary "must" in my life is need is for exercise, which in my pre-anorexic running days was nothing but a hugely beneficial part of my life. Asking me to cut my level of exercise is a gut-wrenching question, but if I address the challenge with some rationale thinking, I'm confident that reducing the amount of time I'm in the water will feel less painful than reducing number of days I head to the pool for a swim.

When Tackling Steps 1 to 4: Go with your Gut

Do your upmost to avoid the natural temptation to over think the questions you're asking yourself. They're pretty simple, so approach them with simplicity in mind.

It's really important that you trust in your instinct by going with your gut feel. More often than not this will provide the right answer! Trust me, the longer you ponder over it, the easier it is for the addict residing within to trick its host. I've fallen for this countless times over the years when attempting to follow other recovery plans. The prescribed approach I was following were probably sound, but each time I found myself laying the foundations of a plan dictated by my anorectic mindset.... which led to nothing but failure.

If, like me, you've got a natural tendency to challenge/understand every element of a problem all at once, steps 1 to 4 may well have left you feeling completely overwhelmed. And, what normally happens when we feel we feel overwhelmed? For those like me, we seek safety by using the harmful behaviours we've become wedded to in a bid to provide what we know is a false sense of control. Try not to let your emotions get the better of you. Treat it like the methodical process that it is!

Step 5

Bring your findings from steps 1 to 4 into a coherent 4-week action plan ….<u>no further</u> into the time horizon for now!

For those who know me well, I f*cking love a good plan!

To begin to weaken the wall standing in front of you (mine has been fortified) a challenging but attainable short-term plan has to be the way to kickstart the necessary momentum of change. Look too far into the future and it runs the risk of setting unattainable goals at this moment in time that do nothing more than freak you (and I) out… leaving us destined to another setback on the road towards recovery.

The overwhelming intention is to take small steps in the right direction, not 'solve world peace' overnight. So, keep it simple and most importantly, achievable! Your plan may only result in a single step, possibly a shuffle forward over the initial 4 weeks. How far you go at the start doesn't matter. The aim here is to create positive momentum that will serve you well over the coming months.

To help you digest everything you've read so far in this chapter I've produced an illustrative example of my personal plan in the next chapter. My doing so, I'm not doing you a favour. Selfishly I need it for me! ☺

Step 6: Possibly the most Important

Muster the courage to lift the lid on the past to build an objective understanding of the life events and/or relationships that could have steered you to where you stand today.

For anyone who's experienced trauma in life, digging deep into your past can be emotionally testing, requiring bravery and an abundance of patience to go through the process properly. Even if a standout event isn't clear, the building blocks to help explain why someone could have led themselves into a world like mine will more often than not sit deep in the past. To build an objective understanding of the past requires a willingness from the outset to revisit the landscape that forms the life picture we've already painted in our heads. This picture can easily be distorted by anger and blame, so we need to be prepared to repaint parts of it.

If you're lucky enough to have already been through a decent stint of psychological therapy, it's likely that a therapist will have helped to gain greater clarity concerning your past. This can be incredibly powerful especially when it comes to understanding the parts of our history that we tend to block out. Not already had this advice from a therapist or currently on a waiting list to see one? By no means does this put you at a disadvantage!

It was 4 years too late before I properly tackled step 6. I put this down to nothing more than carrying the stereotypical mindset of a British man in his 40s, culturally programmed to avoid tackling vulnerability. Whilst my learnings have taught me that I should have entered the abyss of my past a lot sooner, I'd advise anyone wanting to challenge the type of addiction led behaviours that remain in my life by tackling the first 5 steps before even thinking about step 6. It can wait a little while before diving into this one... but sooner than 4 years down the line!

Making changes that challenge those powerful behaviours/thoughts is likely to be difficult enough, having to cope with feelings and emotions that come with feeling like you've lost control. Dealing with this alongside an attempt to understand what events, experiences or relationships may have led you to where you stand today is likely to present an unattainable combined goal. Attempting to do both in parallel goes against the core principle of the overarching themes in the theory we're attempting to apply... small steps!

When the time comes to embark on a journey into our past, it can help to build an unrecognisable amount inner strength that we can take into the future! To help, I've got a few pointers in a bid to help when it comes to tackling step 6:

Start by being clear in your thinking that whatever has happened in the past, there's always a way forward. If actions you've taken or decisions you've made in adult life have been ill-judged, these are now in the past and should stay just there. If experiences dating back to your childhood present the root cause of your present-day challenges, don't fall into the same trap that I did, finding ways to put yourself at fault. Fault, whoever it ultimately sits with is nothing but incidental when it comes to recovery.

Avoid the Blame Game

A frustration of mine concerning the workings of the human brain (well, definitely mine!) is the 'route one' path it initially takes to blame oneself or someone else in your life, today or in the past, for challenges you may face right now. It's hard not to resort to the blame game, which goes against the natural path of thinking. At the same time, I can't emphasise how important it is that you fight the temptation.

I wasted years after my father's death caught up in the blame game. It began with me blaming myself for somehow not being good enough to earn the father/son relationship I desperately wanted as a kid. Then one day a therapist switched on the light in my mind that helped me see that my dad was in the role of parent, and I was simply a child. From there I swiftly moved on to internalise all blame towards him for everything. During the first couple of years battling with anorexia, blaming my dad for everything did nothing more that make me a bitter, angry man who ultimately lost touch with everything good in his life. This anger not only worked to strengthen the relationship I'd built with anorexia it nearly cost me my marriage, my children and ultimately delayed any chance of me being able to make a full recovery.

Take your Time

If you're of a similar mould to me, someone who doesn't have time for any dithering when it comes to solving problems (regardless of complexity), you must be prepared to have your short patience challenged. The easy answer when it comes to trying to understand what could have led us into a dance with mental ill-health is normally to point towards an isolated event, relationship, or a unique set of circumstances. All too often, the conclusion staring straight into our eyes could have been the catalyst, but the underlying cause is less obvious, sitting deep in our past.

In my case, I instantly pointed straight towards the trauma I'd experienced during the final few weeks of my dad's life as the sole cause of the crisis I found myself in. This conclusion had perfectly sound reasoning but proved to be entirely wrong. It took a long time for me to realise my father's passing was merely the trigger event that sparked my downfall. The true underlying cause was the damaged relationship I had with my dad that stemmed all the way back to my early childhood. It was years after my father's death when I finally managed to locate and fit the missing pieces of my 'life' jigsaw into the empty spaces.

Look deep Within

It's not always the case but the source of an encounter with mental ill-health often sits deep in the past. Reflecting now on my own journey which led me to the point that I fell off a cognitive cliff edge, it was an inevitable outcome... more a question of 'when' rather than 'if' I would reach the edge.

A constant and intense desire for recognition from my dad, born out of his somewhat emotionally distant approach to parenting, stemmed all the way back to my earliest memories. This created the person I'd become... I was living with an obsessive fear of failure (and still do, but to a far lesser extent), with a sole focus in life to prove I had a single ounce of worth. My life had become devoted to pleasing everyone else... my boss, work colleagues, family, friends, in-fact anyone I encountered... regardless of whether they actually had a desire to be pleased! Any degree of self-worth I held as a child had evaporated long ago, until I stumbled across the false sense of power that an eating disorder would ultimately provide.

Don't run away from Discomfort

Flight from a perceived threat is a natural human instinct. It's an emotional rollercoaster when entering a journey to map out and understand how past events could help to explain why you've ended up in a difficult place. It's common, just as it was with me, that the anticipation of inner discomfort means we end up running away from the places in our mind that have been locked away for so long.

Whilst ironic, the journey to understand how your past has led you to where you stand right now can actually provide an enormous sense of relief rather than the anticipated discomfort. This in turn can serve as a powerful force to create a brighter future for oneself and of course surrounding loved ones. I'm like every other imperfect parent who makes mistakes every day. But the learnings I've taken from a deep understanding of how my earlier years probably set me on a path to destruction has without doubt helped my broader parenting and the relationship I've got with my own children. In the eyes of my kids, I'm rarely flavour of the month (or day), especially when it comes to my role as 'bad cop', but I sincerely hope that when they reach adulthood, they'll recognise that despite his many faults, their dad was always there for them, no matter what!

Seek Therapy

Securing psychiatric treatment these days is f*cking easier said than done, a catastrophic failure on the part of various governments that doesn't to get the level of media attention it deserves. Already sky high pre-covid psych health NHS waiting lists have now rocketed into outer space since the pandemic. Going private is the alternative but this pathway comes with its own barriers to entry. Few people in the current economic climate are in any position to self-fund a ten session treatment programme. And then there's the largely unrecognised complication that comes with having to navigate through the countless different specialisms just to identify a therapist who can support your specific needs. Sadly, the associated complexity often stops those who simply don't have the cognitive stamina to navigate through the minefield.

Coming out the other side of a successful course of therapy can feel like winning the lottery. Having worked in the industry I'd advise anyone to check whether their employer has an EAP (Employee Assistance Programme). Some employers have it as an employee benefit but fail to publicise the funded access it gives to some form of therapy. If this isn't an option, you must (for your sake) dig deep and go to see your GP.

It's fundamentally wrong that someone in a fragile state of mind should have to fight to secure help, but unfortunately this now the reality for many. If you're in a place where you're unable to muster the strength to demand from your GP that being sent away with a course of antidepressants is simply not acceptable, please ensure you ask a loved one or trusted friend to accompany you. As a minimum it's essential that you at least get on the waiting list! During the waiting period charity support services can perform wonders in terms of connecting communities of like-minded people, all facing similar challenges. In itself, connection can provide great comfort from the realisation that you're not alone!

One simple yet immensely powerful form of self-therapy I'd highly recommend as a brilliant self-soother would be to map out your life journey on paper ... your own interpretation of the events, no matter how small, that could have led you down a path to where you stand today, using nothing but pictures and quotes (be they genuine or what you believe). Sound a bit wet? That's exactly what I thought when this exercise was first recommended to me by a therapist back in 2018. A few weeks later having completed five A3 pages full of detailed drawings (validating why I didn't take GCSE Art!), I stood back for the first time with the feeling that I'd finally made sense of my journey!

Final Points

If you've arrived at the end of this chapter feeling like a dense fog has emersed over your brain, there's absolutely no need to worry. My journey through a heck of a lot of personal sh*t has taken 7 years to arrive at the platform I now stand on. The experience has come with a lot of deep thinking, which I've done my upmost to articulate as best as possible. That said, there's a fair amount of deep sh*t to digest so it may be beneficial to go over it again. This will help to cement the overall structure and supporting themes of the recovery plan. If you're in anyway like me, someone who prefers visuals to accompany text, the next chapter will help build on the picture you've hopefully already started to form.

CHAPTER 15
My Personal Recovery Plan

Fourteen chapters in and it's suddenly dawned on me that my approach taken in what's been my first step into the world of literacy has been well and truly 'ar*e about face'!

Would any respectable author in the world of 'self-help' invest months of their time writing, only to arrive at the halfway point of their latest project and think, "hang on a sec, I haven't actually tested the theory I've been banging on about?" I think we both know the answer! An author of the saner variety would be far more sensible, starting by testing the logic to establish whether it's worth actually investing any time writing! But hey, I'm a genuine novice, and if I we're of the saner variety I'd have never encountered the parts of my history that sparked the initial idea to write in the first place!

Before I actually test what is at this stage an entirely conceptual and therefore unproven recovery model, I'll do as I promised at the end of the last chapter by setting out my own, currently unactioned recovery plan. This will cover the first 5 of the 6 steps laid out in the last chapter. Why only the first 5 steps? Because my journey to this point started with step 6 (understanding my past) which I guess does nothing more than reinforce my 'ar*se about face' approach! On a more serious note, if you're literally starting from ground zero on your journey, remember the guidance I've already given ... start by embedding some of those small changes before even considering an attempt to tackle step 6. Proving that you can make positive changes will build the essential strength and cognitive balance needed to start unpicking the preceding journey that's seen you arrive at platform you stand on today.

My Recovery Plan

Steps 1 + 2: My Primary & Secondary Addiction "Musts"

PRIMARY MUSTS	I absolutely **must** hit my daily exercise target 2 hours minimum	I **must** stay within the **strict** boundaries of 'allowable' foods
SECONDARY MUSTS	I **must** not eat before my allotted mealtimes Breakfast: 11:00 Lunch: 15:00 Dinner: 21:00	I **must** have a beer and glass of wine every evening

Step 3: Frequency / Severity of my **Primary** "Musts"

	FREQUENCY	SEVERITY
EXERCISE TARGET	High intensity physical exercise (minimum 6 days each week) Daily low intensity physical exercise (e.g. walking the dog)	40 minutes high intensity workout 60 minutes low intensity workout (Both flex to hit 2 hour target)
ALLOWABLE FOOD	Stay within the **strict** boundaries of allowable foods with exception of my Saturday night takeaway	Maximum of 2500 calories per day (Weekly average)

Step 4: Identify the Primary "Must" Elements **I will** challenge

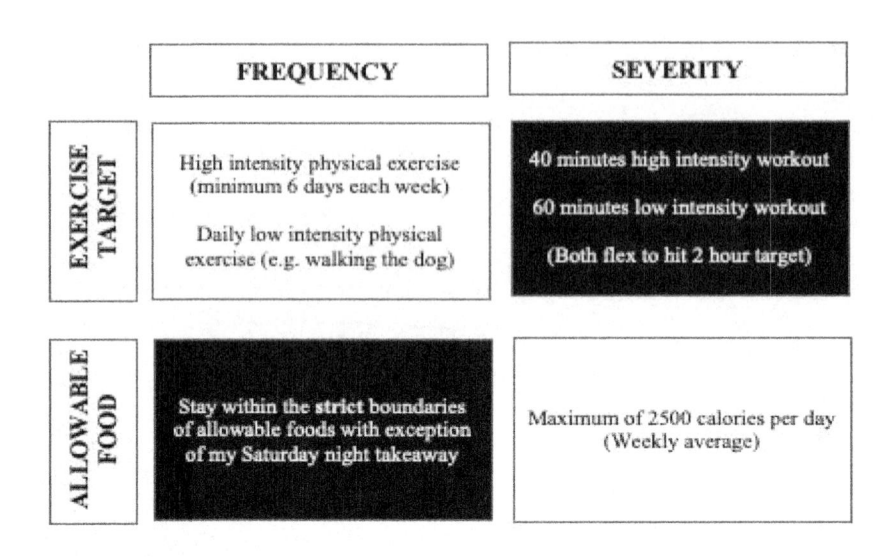

	FREQUENCY	**SEVERITY**
EXERCISE TARGET	High intensity physical exercise (minimum 6 days each week) Daily low intensity physical exercise (e.g. walking the dog)	**40 minutes high intensity workout** **60 minutes low intensity workout** **(Both flex to hit 2 hour target)**
ALLOWABLE FOOD	**Stay within the strict boundaries of allowable foods with exception of my Saturday night takeaway**	Maximum of 2500 calories per day (Weekly average)

Highlighted Sections = Targeted areas

Step 5: My 4 Week Plan: Targeted Outcomes

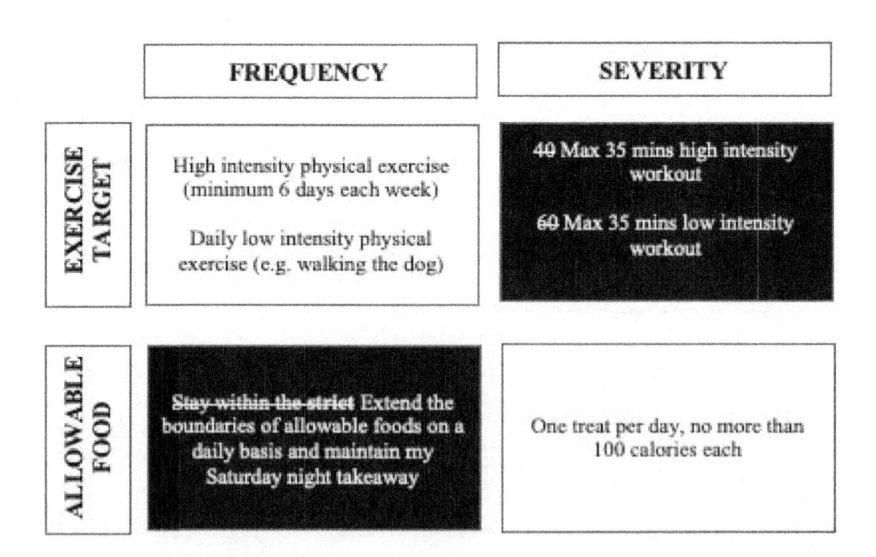

	FREQUENCY	**SEVERITY**
EXERCISE TARGET	High intensity physical exercise (minimum 6 days each week) Daily low intensity physical exercise (e.g. walking the dog)	**40 Max 35 mins high intensity workout** **60 Max 35 mins low intensity workout**
ALLOWABLE FOOD	**~~Stay within the strict~~ Extend the boundaries of allowable foods on a daily basis and maintain my Saturday night takeaway**	One treat per day, no more than 100 calories each

There are two things that I **absolutely** have to get clear in my head right from the outset:

1. The extent to which I can/should challenge the "musts" from day one... **too soon will end in failure.**

How far I actually get over the 8 weeks should have no bearing on my perception of achievement... **a handful of steps forward will create the momentum for more down the line.**

After 7 years living with a mind locked in solitary confinement, I actually don't give a f*ck how long the process takes. I also fully accept there will be the usual eb and flow of bad vs better days. As I enter the test, I feel confident that for once my innate sense of urgency has been tempered, having shaken hands with my subconscious on the reality that the goals I've set cannot be achieved overnight. A successful outcome from however many 4-week cycles of change it ends up taking is actually pretty damn simple:

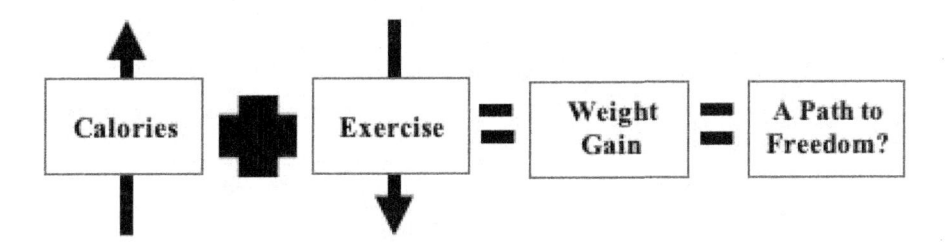

$$\text{Calories} \uparrow + \text{Exercise} \downarrow = \text{Weight Gain} = \text{A Path to Freedom?}$$

A formula that to be frank does little more than spell out the bl**dy obvious to anyone with an ounce of common sense! Consuming more calories and reducing exercise will always lead to weight gain, especially when the body is already crying out to replenish depleted cells. Really f*cking simple, but critical if I'm to stand any chance of moving on to pastures new.

The end outcome is exactly the same as that from following the standard abstinence recovery model. The key difference (in theory) is the greater chance this approach gives to maintain one's ability to continue functioning during a cycle of challenging change. With this should come a dramatically improved chance of long-term success (versus the 'cold turkey' approach).

I know the next few weeks are going to be f*cking tough! Any change to my routine, no matter how small, will drive a backlash from my highly entrenched mindset. I'm expecting setbacks along the way which means I need to accept from the outset that the plan I've set isn't a hard one. I can and will adjust as I learn through the experience, adapting as needed when presented with one of those unforeseen challenges that life tends to throw at all of us.

From here on, building and maintaining a momentum of change will only be possible if I stay loyal to the principle that small improvements will eventually snowball into bigger ones.

So here goes….

PROGRESS?

CHAPTER 16
+2.8kg

A month on since finishing the last chapter! I'd like to say it was an intentional break, but the reality is that I've found it virtually impossible to muster any sense of motivation or creativity to build on the foundations already laid. This is the point I should find a convenient excuse as a means to explain… work? family distractions? Both fronts have been as hectic as ever, including a steady stream of 12+ hour working days over recent weeks. But I'd be lying if I were to place the blame at the door of either. The truth is the break has been down to the overwhelming distraction from the changes I've been making to my cemented daily addiction led routine. Honesty is an attribute that resides deep within my DNA. With this comes an acknowledgment that the few first steps I'd planned to help me move me towards a place where I (not anorexia) can call the shots has been far harder and energy sapping than first thought. But hey, if it we're easy to fix the hardwired thoughts, feelings and behaviours that come with 'addiction' the word would be an alien concept!

I never invited addiction into my world. But having failed to spot it creep in through the unlocked back door, the core attributes of the illness have systematically taken a hold on every part of my life and those around me, spreading like ivy with the sole purpose to attach then strangulate everything in its path. With me choosing to ignore the problem over the years since that initial diagnosis, the concrete foundations laid by anorexia have hardened and built upon with each passing year. I live in hope that fellow addicts may read this book and learn from the mistakes I've made, with any luck finding a way to break free far sooner than me… which of course remains something I'm yet to achieve!

Over the past few weeks, I've painstakingly tried to make

changes I'd planned, but if truth be known, it's felt like trying to break through the wall of a reinforced prison cell armed with nothing but a blunt utensil… leaving me with no option but to chip and scrape away the brick dust. Addicts (like me) become professionals at kidding ourselves that it'll easy to kick the habit, but "it can wait until tomorrow". And with that, the tomorrow we truly yearn for never actually arrives. But as things stand, whilst the utopian tomorrow remains in the distance, I am starting to feel a fresher dawn breaking.

The last month has proved to be nothing but a f*cking slog, my mind wholly preoccupied with driving towards the ultimate lifestyle changes I've set out to achieve, leaving little to no desire for writing. BUT… I've actually made progress, maybe to the extent that a single brick in the lining of that cell wall has been dislodged, revealing a narrow ray of light from the other side!

75.8kg

At the start of my first of what could prove to be a number of 4-week plans, I made the conscious decision to remain patient by waiting until the end to weigh myself. With today marking the end of 'cycle 1' I nearly fell off the scales when they registered, the distance between the platform and the bathroom floor feeling like I was looking over a cliff edge…75.8kg (11 stone 13lb in 'old money')!!! Sound light for a guy measuring in at 6'3" (around 193cm in 'new money')? Probably the easiest question you'll answer all year but having spent the last 3 years carrying a stagnated body mass, this presents as a landmark moment for me, finally reaching my prime pre-anorexia running weight… although no way near capable of running a 3-hour marathon!

How has the news left me feeling? If truth be known, with mixed emotions… a small sense of adulation that my plan could actually be working, yet petrified that once started, the weight gain will continue into perpetuity (the biggest fear for any anorectic). Physically, it's hard to assess whether the growth in body mass has made any real difference which I guess is hardly surprising given it represents a mere +3% of weight gain. The ultimate challenge will come from the anorectic voice, wholly incapably of connecting any change with its accompanying scale, resulting in an inevitable backlash aligned to doubling my weight!!

As soon as the scales registered this morning my anorexic 'friend' instantaneously kicked into life. From there I was left simultaneously fighting a never-ending flow of insults from within whilst trying to remain focused on a demanding job… as I write now, I feel near to cognitively broken… "you fat f*cker!", "can you feel that tracker tyre hanging over your belt?" … blah, blah, f*cking blah!.

If the truth be known, bringing out the utter madness of my anorectic thinking over the course of the preceding chapters has kinda prepared me for the guaranteed eating disorder counter offensive. Over the years I've always ended up relenting to the demands of the voice, immediately resorting to weight loss tactics. Whilst I've certainly felt more prepared this time around for the onslaught, past experience still begs the question "will I manage to cope?". That said, whilst it's felt far from a walk in the park this time around, the experience hasn't felt quite as arduous as the past has taught me.

A few years back I spent a year or so attending regular appointments with a Tunbridge Wells (Kent) based therapist. Bernie Wright was, and from what I still read on LinkedIn, remains an amazing professional, devoting her working life to supporting people like me and doing everything within her power to raise the profile of a growing UK eating disorder epidemic. Alongside benefiting from that genuine, not monetary driven desire to help others, my resounding takeaway from the time we spent together was her careful, yet powerful use of words, always replacing "weight" with "health" when discussing my need for more. Such a subtle difference but her use of language in this way always hit home, even in the very dark days living in the strangulating clasp of the illness. I often reflect with a sense of regret that no matter how good Bernie was, I simply couldn't find the strength to change my pattern of living, the inner anorectic voice too loud and controlling which curtailed any chance of a shift in behaviour.

The truth is that whilst the recent gains I've made in my spectrum of "health" are 'marginal', making it impossible to see and feel from one day to the next, a little reflection tells me that 5lb has definitely shifted the dial a notch.

Aside from the now month-long battle with the anorectic voice, the only other negative I can attach to what I hope is the start of a body and mind transformation, would be the sheer exhaustion that's accompanied my small increase in 'health'. Admittedly based on zero scientific evidence, I'm putting this down to my weakened immune system, battered by years of semi-starvation, suddenly sprung into overdrive, desperately trying to replenish the essential cells my body has had no choice but to manage without over the years.

In contrast, the positive effects of just 5lb in additional "health" are clear as I write now:

Nourishment

I've started eating foods I once loved but spent years petrified of. The light switch is yet to be turned on to full illumination (i.e., I'm not spending all day troughing on chocolate and biscuits nor gorging on takeaways every night). It's more akin to a dimmer switch turned on at its lowest setting, providing just enough light to be able to move around without going a*se over face.

I'm now sampling different tastes and textures (in small quantities) that I've not experienced for a long time.... peanut butter, full fat crisps, takeaway curry (only one managed so far), chips, Yorkshire pudding and grilled haloumi to name a few.... None of it healthy on the heart, but definitely proving healthy for my mind!

The Voice

Whilst the anorectic voice hasn't packed up its belongings and left my mind, it has weakened a little. The balance of power still resides with the eating disorder but on handful of occasions over the past month I've been able crush the voice...something that's been impossible in the past.

Observing Life

Likely to be a mix of the placebo effect from the sense of achievement, and of course the extra nourishment my brain has received, I've found myself noticing and appreciating life around me a little more. Take walking the dog as a means to illustrate. Cooper and I often venture for a walk along a local country bridleway, lined with trees and fields that stretch as far as the distant horizon. I'd normally head down there with 'Coops' with nothing on my mind but how far I could walk (to burn calories) or how long I could stay out (to avoid any temptation to eat at home). With autumn now upon us, I've found myself focusing on the beauty from the vast array of colours this season rewards us with, able to tell the anorectic voice to f*ck-off the moment it starts to pipe up. Most important of all, I'm seeing the sheer amount of excitement in 'Coops' as he runs free, taking advantage of the opportunity it gives him to satisfy his desire for new scents, meet and play with other dogs, and of course, dive into the odd field to chase down a pheasant (always without success!).

Stress Management

Whilst my consistently long working hours over recent months have conflicted heavily with the aspiration to carry a positive sense of professional wellbeing, I'd say that I'm coping far better than before. Maybe the additional nourishment has left me with a greater cognitive balance, providing essential strength to deal with challenges in a more rational way.

All of the above have played also played part in making homelife feel better than it's been for years. Family life hasn't been in a bad place for a few years now, but I'd be lying if I didn't acknowledge that all of the anorectic restrictions and demands have left it rather stale at times… something I will feel a sense of guilt about until the day my time is up. Whilst it's not been perfect, just like any family with parents desperately trying to keep their kids on the straight and narrow, I'd say that it's improved a lot recently. I've found myself laughing far more with my wife and children, although I'm sure the embarrassing dad act is starting to leave my kids wishing that 'serious' dad would return ☺.

BUT…

I have taken some positive steps forward to widen and extend my nutritional intake, but I'm keeping my feet firmly on the ground in the knowledge that not all areas of intended change have gone according to the original plan. Whilst I've managed to make some small inroads to reduce my exercise pattern, the urge remains just as powerful as it did a month ago. Despite this, I take comfort from the fact that I've not responded to the threat from consuming additional calories as I once would have, by compensating with a ramp up in strenuous exercise.

With Christmas around the corner, presenting a whole new world of additional challenges for those living with eating disorders (see next chapter), I'm not beating myself up over any small gaps in progress. I knew from the outset this would be a journey that would take time and patience to get to the end point. For now, I'm giving myself a gentle pat on the back as a reward for the 5lb gain in "health", which appears to have opened the door to some subtle improvements to my daily life. There's still a long way to go before I can even contemplate celebrating, so my focus has to remain firmly fixed on ploughing through the festive period with a little momentum, then seek to address any gaps in change following the turn of the new year.

SEASON'S GREETINGS

FFS, please get this starving 'wannabe' a box… actually no… a f*cking crate of mince pies!

"To make mistakes is human; to stumble is commonplace; to be able to laugh at yourself is maturity"

William Arthur Ward

CHAPTER 17
Merry F*cking Christmas

Christmas, the time of year enjoyed by all… family gatherings, parties with friends/work colleagues, and of course, the magic created by the imagination of younger 'believers' which spreads to the parents who reminisce about the excitement that Christmas once brought to them. A time when family and friends gather to eat, drink and be merry, regardless of faith. Everyone loves Christmas, don't they?

Certain circumstances can make the reality of Christmas play out as the polar opposite to the portrayal of warmth and harmony we see on the annual John Lewis festive advert. Loneliness and coping with a recently lost loved one would be the standout markers, but there are lesser-known circumstances that can make the festive period hellish for some.

I've unintentionally used this book as a platform to become the self-appointed Head of the UK's 'Union of Addicts'! With this in mind I'd be doing my members a complete disservice if I failed to call out that many of them will far from relish the thought of Christmas approaching. Why? Because for many addicts (like me), however hard we may try to hide from Christmas, the fuel that can reignite self-harming behaviours is served up in abundance during December. All too often, this can easily lead to a month of crippling anxiety led torment.

If you're an alcoholic trying to break the cycle, you're faced with our very British way of celebrating… everything involves alcohol! If you're a gambling addict, what is undoubtably the busiest part of the domestic sporting calendar presents a Christmas bonus opportunity for the bookies with all forms of media plagued with enticing adverts promoting free bets and boosted odds. If you're an anorectic (like me), you're faced with an abundance of the thing you fear the most … copious amounts food, in just about every category that sit firmly outside the boundaries of acceptability (apart from the sprouts ☺!). When the 12 days have been and gone it doesn't stop there for anorectics, then plagued by countless new year diet fads promoted by C list celebrities. These do nothing but excite the devil from within, serving up tempting new ways to restrict nutrition!

It may come across like I'm putting a massive downer on a time of year that brings joy to the majority (once upon a time, including myself). I can assure you this isn't my intention. Afterall, life is hard enough over the other 353 days of the year without some 'do-gooder wellbeing advocate' trying to spoil the party. I'm merely attempting to create a wider awareness of the largely unknown, often invisible, yet insurmountable challenge faced all kinds of addicts at Christmas. These people **desperately** want to enjoy the festive magic but any chance of this becoming a reality is stopped dead by the crippling illness they carry.

Until the ripe old age of 36 I always enjoyed the festive period. Christmas parties with work colleagues (followed by a stinking hanger), a few pints down the pub with friends on Christmas eve (potent 'winter warmer' ale tasting better than any beer consumed during the summer months), a massive Christmas roast (followed by seconds), and of course, the essential turkey and pickle sarnie (on thick white bread) in the evening. As I finish this paragraph, I can actually feel a sentimental warmth starting to rise from deep within my core!

Since 2014, Christmas has been nothing hell, presenting nothing but a huge challenge to my all-round stability. Back in 2014, just after my father's passing in the September, I found myself in the depths of a mental health crisis. My wife, children, then aged 6 and 3, and I, went to my aunt and uncle's house on Christmas Day for a big family get together. By this point, a little under 4 months after my dad had died, I'd become a mere shell of my former self, emaciated and utterly exhausted having battered myself from simultaneously running 100+ miles week whilst heavily restricting my calorie intake. As always, my wife showed remarkable strength, putting a brave face on for the kids, doing everything she could to give them the magic of Christmas they deserved. In the years since 2014 anorexia has restricted me to a small handful of fond festive memories, missing the hundreds of others my wife holds. I can't even put the absence of memories down to not being able to see my children. The blame lies firmly at the door of the self-centered illness that removed me from any sense of reality.

The annual festivities have improved since that first 'anorexic' Christmas, but in large, they've remained pretty miserable. What comes with being unable to re-write history is regret, my biggest being that despite the effort to hide my heightened state of anxiety, there was tense atmosphere felt by everyone at home (who deserved to enjoy themselves!).

Christmas would kick-off for me as soon as December registered on the calendar. The opening of the first window on my kid's advent calendars would spark fear in what could eventually come on that single day of the year, Christmas Day. Although to a lesser extent these days, the clock striking midnight, signaling the arrival of December 1st, still creates an instantaneous, overpowering compulsion to over exercise. Why? To overcompensate for what I could face on the 25th!

Since 2014, I'm certain in saying that I've sat in an extreme minority of people… those who actually lose weight over Christmas. By the time the big day arrives, I'd historically have smashed myself to pieces with excessive running or swimming, just to allow myself that extra 1000 calories on the big day. A case of sheer f*cking madness at all levels, but the like-minded among us will understand.

One of the few positive Christmas memories I've managed to

retain from recent years has to be when I dressed up as Santa (pictured). I don't recall exactly how old my kids were, but I'd say they were probably 6 and 9. I'd somehow managed get my hands on what I can only describe as the Ferrari of Santa suits, arranging with my wife that I'd be at the top of our cul-de-sac at 8pm, three pillows stuffed into the mid-rift of the suit in an attempt to give me some desperately needed mass. Bang on 8pm my wife "heard something" and quickly gathered with my kids at the upstairs window. Upon opening the window my son, then 3, was screaming in delight having just seen Santa. My daughter, sharp as the best razor blade money can buy, turned round to my wife, and said, "isn't that daddy?". To be fair, I made a cr*p Santa... 6'3" and weighing in at under 70kg... but hey, I look back now and see the funny side!

This year, as we approach the big day it's felt a little different to years gone by. The challenges I've come to expect at this time of year still arrived in their usual timely manner, but they haven't felt quite as bad as in days gone by. YES, I have swam more than usual this month, but it's not been out of control as it was previous years. YES, I did miss the work Christmas party, the first since the pandemic, but this wasn't down to a decision to avoid it (I had Covid – again!). At the same time, NO, I haven't been shi**ing myself throughout December at the thought having to tackle Christmas Day, remaining pretty relaxed about it as I write now on Christmas Eve. And NO, I've not restricted my nutritional intake, choosing to go with the flow as much as possible, for my family's sake, evening suggesting we get a Chinese takeaway on the way back from a recent family ice skating jolly. I'm determined that whilst I know that Christmas will remain far from perfect this year (although I'm not entirely clear what that really looks like in the real world), it will represent a marked improvement on those we've had over recent years!

The Big Day

It's now 20:30 and we've just arrived home from a day at the in-law's, meaning Christmas Day is finally drawing to a close. All in all, it's actually been a half decent day with anxiety largely kept to a bare minimum.

The day kicked off with the kids waking us up at 8am, the only day this year that my 14-year-old daughter has managed to surface before 11am on a non-school day! Stockings emptied, presents under the tree opened and the dog walked, it was off to my wife's parents in Caterham (Surrey). We arrived at midday, me waiting with bated breath for the question I yearned to be asked by my father-in-law... "Fancy a pint?".

Next stop, The King and Queen, a local Fullers pub, with Cooper in tow (the dog loves a good pub). An opportunity for a couple (well, two and a half) pints of the king of cask ales, ESB... smooth but strong (just like me – don't f*cking laugh!). Christmas Day in the UK isn't the same without an early afternoon stroll down to the local pub, everyone in good spirit, strangers engaging in conversation as if they'd known each other for years. I rarely get the chance to visit the great British mecca that is one's local pub, so really enjoy the couple of hours sat by the fire with a pint and the dog, managing to hold my own as the solitary Chelsea fan among a heavily weighted contingent of (Crystal) Palace supporters. The clock strikes 14:30 and with final orders approaching the taste for beer left me pondering over the catalogue 'man' excuses to justify a final pint... but with dinner being served at 15:00, the father-in-law and I play it safe, avoiding the risk of a strong ticking off from my mother-in-law... plus I'd volunteered to drive back home this evening.

In Christmases gone by, I'd have been absolutely shi**ing myself from the moment I woke right up until dinner was served. Even a trip to the pub would do nothing to dull the anxiety. But this year has felt different. I'd promised myself a decent Christmas dinner, something I've consistently done but failed to achieve over recent years, the difference this year that it wasn't a false promise! The anorectic voice was there throughout the day, but carried far less weight, allowing me to put away a decent plate of beef, turkey, roast potatoes, veg and stuffing, followed by the only desert that should be eaten on the December 25th... rich and fruity Christmas Pudding... my first in 9 years!

When I think back to the level of indulgence I'd partake in over festive periods pre anorexia, this year has been relatively low key. But the goal this year wasn't to completely rip up the rule book of the unhealthy mind. It was to get through the day having achieved gains without derailing myself. Mission accomplished!

CTFC

Boxing day arrives and for the first year in a long as I can recall, I wake up without the guilt-ridden regret from a false perception of over consumption. That said, with the leisure centre shut (meaning no option for a swim), I head out for... guess what... a run! Now's the time when a therapist would destroy me (in a nice way), for succumbing to the inner "musts". I wouldn't knock their sentiment, but this time, I was in control... 30 minutes, not a second longer.

Why did I decide to ignore my addiction "musts" yelling at me to attempt a half marathon for old times sake? Aside from my inability now to cover the distance, having stopped running ages ago, I had a date planned with my daughter. With a fully loaded Boxing Day football fixture list, we head to Crawley Town FC to watch them play a league 2 match against Sutton Utd. Yes, I may be born and breed Chelsea, but Crawley are local and there's something special these days about the game nearer to the grassroots end of football, sparking memories of Saturday afternoons at Stamford Bridge in the 80's... normal, everyday working people turning out to support their team, grab a pie and sink a couple of pints with their mates… a country mile away from all the prawn sarnies and client entertaining we now see at Premier League games!

Despite Crawley Town going down to a 2-1 defeat and being forced to prize our backsides off the ice block seats at full time, dad and daughter had a good time together… although she couldn't understand the concept of drinking hot Bovril! Given the time I dedicate to my son's football team, which usually clashes with my daughter's gymnastics, dad/daughter 121 time is rare. I loved spending time with her, but if truth be known, I'm not sure the feeling was mutual… spending most of the game eyeing up the talent on the pitch!

House Party

Our festive period finally ended at 3am this morning (30th December). New Year's Eve has never been a big night for us, so it's likely to be a quiet one tomorrow… plus, given the way I'm feeling right now with the aftereffects from attempting to drink like a 21 year old again last night, I'm not sure I'd be capable of 'going again' in a little over 24 hours' time.

My two half-sisters, accompanied by other halves, came over to ours for a BBQ (yes, in December), followed by a night of games and way too much beer. The eldest of my two sisters is 13 years younger than me, and with both of them still enjoying the freedom of life without kids, they remain firmly sat in the party stage of life. Despite the challenges I had with my/our dad, something we rarely talk about, we've remained close, although like many family relationships, we fail to see each other anywhere near as often as we should.

A load of bland context with no real relationship with the broader theme of this book? Be patient! Over recent years, amongst other things, I'd describe myself as a semi-social hermit, usually doing my upmost to avoid a high tempo social situation. Why? Because they're unpredictable and pose a threat to my ability to adhere to the hard-wired addiction "musts" I use to fell that (false) sense of control. Barring the time during the height of the pandemic when it was forced upon us, I've pretty much spent the last 7 years socially locked up. But on the rare occasion I've pitched up to a gathering, it's proved to be far from fun. Last night was different... I genuinely had a great evening... although, sat here now with a stinking hangover, my body is far from thanking me for letting my hair down!

Epiphany

The 'Feast of Epiphany' marks the end of the 12 days of Christmas, celebrating the revelation that Jesus was the son of God... the power of Google, not learnings from my childhood years attending Sunday School.

I can't help but feel a small sense of irony between how I reflect on this festive period which is finally drawing to a close and the use of the word's "feast" and "epiphany" linked to the celebration that Christians mark to end Christmas. Christmas this year hasn't quite been the feast I'd enjoy each and every year pre anorexia, but compared to more recent years, I've enjoyed the opportunity to 'consume' on a whole new level this year. I have pushed myself harder than ever and managed somehow to remain relaxed at Christmas for the first time in years... maybe this year been my mini revelation?

If you've read this chapter and drawn parallels with the annual festive challenge articulated, I'd urge you to dig deep the next time Christmas approaches to find that fraction of strength from within that could help avoid you repeating the same mistakes I've made. Those years were lost to addiction, never to be seen again, with me left left blind to the magic Christmas created for my young children and the chance of it gave my surrounding family to relax and enjoy the experience. I can't get those years back, but you stand a chance of avoiding the same happening to you!

If like me, you've already lost countless Christmases to a dark distraction, I sincerely hope my experience this year helps inspire you when the next one arrives. Regret over what's happened in the past is the easiest way to stay in the past. 'Groundhog Day', the iconic 1980s US comedy starring Bill Murray, springs to mind… a film that becomes pretty f*cking boring when it gets to the fourth cycle of the same bl**dy scenes. Don't let the next festive period become your next Groundhog Day!

THE INSANE MODERN WORLD

&

PATHOLOGICAL NARCISSIM

CHAPTER 18
Is Today's World Leaving Us More F*cked Up Than Ever Before?

My Soapbox Moment!

If you're one of the growing number of people in today's world, cut off from reality by the bubble created by social media, or simply been too damn busy to notice, we (notably in the west) are in the midst of a genuine and growing mental health crisis!

Is this crisis a new phenonium, or has it always been there, hidden underground in the past through fear of stigma?

A plethora of different arguments exist, all attempting to explain this critical issue facing society, with consequences carrying far wider than the health of each person effected. The fact is that we're all paying for it, especially in terms of the impact it has on the economic prospects of a nation in a global economy... lower workforce productivity = un-competitive industries = stagnated economic growth = erosion of personal wealth!

Many argue that the problem has always existed but more recently we've seen the lid finally lifted on the topic of mental ill-health due to a shift in societal acceptance that both body and mind can malfunction. This in turn has seen a previously stigmatised group of people finally open up about their cognitive vulnerability.

Others resort to what I see as the easy option to explain the root cause of the issue we're seeing in the UK, placing blame firmly at the door of a sub-standard NHS service that's failed to treat the problem, driven by a of lack of funding and sub-standard management. A plausible argument but it fails to recognise the added pressure on public services from increased demand (i.e., a greater proportion of the population seeking help). From my experience the frailty of NHS mental health services is a gigantic issue, but far from root the cause! Having worked in the private health insurance sector I've seen with my own eyes how the demand for mental health related treatment has exploded in the few years following the pandemic. I'll touch on the impact of Covid-19 later in this chapter, but yet again, it's I'd say that it's also too easy to blame society's current mind health crisis solely on the pandemic. Without doubt it played a significant part, but the main outcome from the pandemic was to expose a fundamentally broken NHS in desperate need of root and branch change.

There's a natural human tendency to look for the easy answer when attempting to explain a complex problem. With this usually comes a degree of disappointment that the root cause of this growing societal challenge doesn't sit behind a single door. The reality (in my opinion) is that the answer is extremely complex, containing multiple, interrelated factors… just like a perfectly formed Venn diagram!

Personal experiences, usually those that stem way back to childhood and adolescent years can play heavily into one's propensity to an encounter with mental ill-health during life, occasionally dished up with a side order of addiction. A lived-in experience of acute mental ill-health alongside a shed load of therapy doesn't only give someone like me an entirely different perspective of their own life, it can open up a wider perspective of the world that surrounds us.

I strongly believe that aspects of societal change witnessed over the last two decades, some of which we've embraced with open arms, have without doubt contributed to the escalating mind-health crisis we're witnessing. In this chapter, I'll lay out my take on the primary causes, some of which are absolute 'slam dunks', others a little more subjective and possibly dependent on one's political stance. So, let's roll my cuboid that returns an 'S' every time, each side representing one of the key shortcomings in modern society I believe is f*cking us up more and more as time passes by:

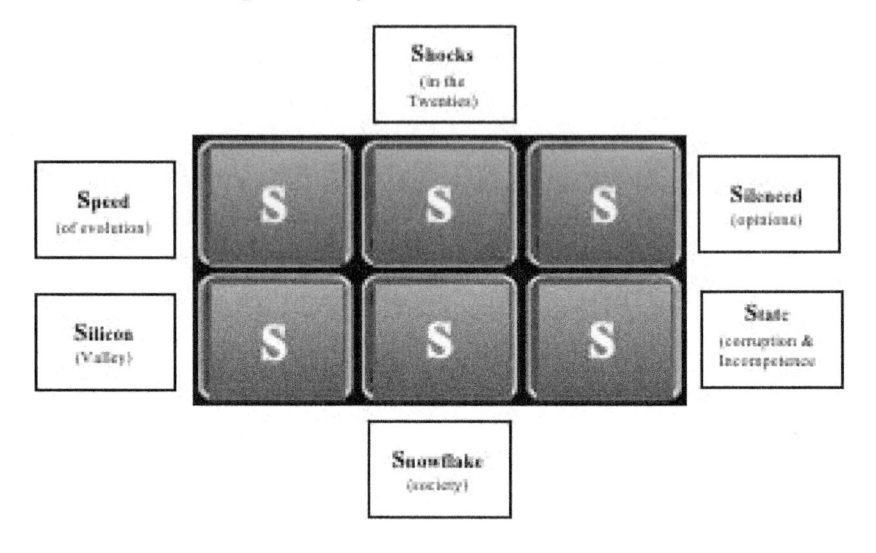

```
                    ┌─────────────┐
                    │   Shocks    │
                    │   (in the   │
                    │  Twenties)  │
                    └─────────────┘
┌──────────┐  ┌─────┐┌─────┐┌─────┐  ┌──────────┐
│  Speed   │  │     ││     ││     │  │ Silenced │
│   (of    │  │  S  ││  S  ││  S  │  │(opinions)│
│evolution)│  │     ││     ││     │  │          │
└──────────┘  └─────┘└─────┘└─────┘  └──────────┘
┌──────────┐  ┌─────┐┌─────┐┌─────┐  ┌──────────┐
│          │  │     ││     ││     │  │  State   │
│ Silicon  │  │  S  ││  S  ││  S  │  │(corruption &│
│ (Valley) │  │     ││     ││     │  │incompetence)│
└──────────┘  └─────┘└─────┘└─────┘  └──────────┘
                    ┌─────────────┐
                    │  Snowflake  │
                    │  (society)  │
                    └─────────────┘
```

Speed (of modern-day evolution)

Over the last decade our day-to-day living has been changing at an ever-greater pace, which I believe has left a section of society struggling to cope. I've not yet concluded in my own mind whether this issue is down to plain old human stupidity (a section of society I firmly sit in!) or simply because the speed of change is conflicting with our brains, hardwired from centuries of steady evolution. Either way, I'm firm in the opinion that it has left some positioned like a rabbit staring into the fast-approaching headlights on a dark country lane!

Our need to constantly evolve is a cornerstone of human DNA. For centuries our way of life has been in a constant state of change, using science and technology to deliver better standards of living and health. This in turn has facilitated seismic growth in the human population, which recently hit 8 billion (in 2023), supporting a totally unrecognisable concept in everyday human thinking that an expansion in our numbers is driven an innate need to guarantee the survival of humankind.

The speed of change that until more recently humankind has managed to cope with has been increasing for centuries. But at the turn of the 21st century an all-mighty turbo was added to the world engine! Rapid change, particularly in the technology we use, has been sold to us as a means to simplify and bring convenience to everyday life. But some people, those possibly carrying a more binary approach to life, have been left struggling to deal with the pace of change in a rational way. In summary, it's left some people struggling to maintain control of the vehicle in the journey towards their final destination (the end of life).

A load of cr*p? Quite possibly but hold that thought until you've at least given me a chance to articulate my point. It's hardly fair for you to dismiss my point without giving me the chance to explain, this presenting a societal trait we've seen emerge over the last decade that I'll observe in more detail later on in this chapter ☺!

Middle to long distance running was once my go-to form of escapism, a pastime I formed a strong bond with, until the onset of anorexia weaponised it against me. I still enjoy watching competitive road and track events which sparked an off-piste attempt to use a running theme as a means to illustrate my point concerning the pace of human evolution since the turn of the 20th century. How?... by relating the societal change over the past century (and a bit) to the epic men's 5000m final at the London 2012 Olympic games… a race that has go down ss one of the best of all time!

I can still remember that day as if were only yesterday, me simultaneously twitching around on the edge of sofa whilst screaming at the TV, hoping that the legendary Mo Farah who played the tactics of his life to destroy a world-class field of middle-distance athletes, would in somehow hear me. I can still see the expression on my 4-year-old daughter's face, staring at me with a bemused look on her face. She clearly thought (in her own little way) that her dad had completely lost the plot which begs the question, did she have a premunition, able to see my ultimate cognitive end state on the horizon, a mere two years later!

12.5 laps of the track, each lap representing a decade in time since the turn of the twentieth century. At 13 minutes 41 seconds, what proved to be a race of tactics, was some way off world record pace, but light years ahead of my respectable 19 minutes 5 second 5k personal best. The first 400 metres clocked in at 74.1 seconds, with race pace at 2km (5 laps in) down to a steady 70 seconds per lap. From that point the pace cranked up, hitting 62 second laps which then continued until the final 2 laps. At this point the nation witnessed that what would become the famous Mo 'kick' that saw him leave the rest of the field behind. Mo ran the last lap of that electrifying final in 52.9 seconds, crossing the line to win gold. To this day, 'Sir Mo' remains an absolute legend in my eyes, only pipped to a very close second place by the 'magical' noughties Chelsea forward, Gianfranco Zola.

In my **very simple** mind, the electrifying pace of Mo's final lap is akin to the extent of change the world has had to cope with over the last full decade (2010-2019).

Let me attempt to illustrate…

Like most parents in their 40's my kids think I'm tech dinosaur, no different what I thought about my parents and grandparents when questioned why I'd disconnect myself from all reality at a family gathering to channel every ounce of mind energy in a bid to level up on Tetris. That iconic first edition Nintendo Gameboy, which I managed to get my hands on at the age of 14, was the introduction to portable gaming back in the 90's. Forget the usual 'brick' analogy, the original Gameboy was more like a f*cking paving slab!

No one can doubt that the advancement of technology/science over the last two decades has outstripped the progression over the entire double century that came before it. I see this advancement as a double-edged sword, the blunt side without doubt being the increasingly sophisticated use of innovation to benefit humankind. There are many examples I could use to articulate how tech has and continues to be used for the better. Take stem cell research as a random example, with advancements in this area of research expected to drive transformational change across the spectrum of global healthcare. Who would have ever envisaged a few years ago that science and technology would enable us to unlock the key to extract basic cells capable of growing into vital organs? F*cking amazing!!

The sharp side of the sword, that without doubt has and continues to fuel the rise in mental ill-health can pooled into a single category known as as 'the internet of things'... this being the multitude of 'smart' mobile devices that have become just as critical for survival as a beating heart. A ridiculous statement? Well read on.

In a multitude of different ways, the world wide web, a gift from Tim Berners-Lee back in 1990, gifted humankind with a third arm. Possibly the most ridiculous metaphor you've ever read before? It has to be up there with the worst, but I'm afraid it's the ceiling of this accountant's creativity whilst attempting to hammer home my point... that 30 years on from the birth of the web, there's absolutely no way we could survive without it! It's given us a multi-tasking capability to manage every part day-to-day life, access to an unlimited wealth of information (although separating fact from fiction is becoming increasingly difficult), and a connection to friends and family wherever they are in the world. All of this from the comfort of a living room sofa!

Have we chosen wisely to reinvest the additional capacity created by the convenience the web has brought to our lives in our own wellbeing? For an increasing proportion of society, the answer would be a resounding no! I've no doubt that an increasing number of us are unknowingly becoming disconnected from the real world, withdrawing from those basic, yet critical human needs like in-person interaction, discussion, and debate, replacing them with an isolated existence on social media.

If you're a parent (like me), you'll probably relate to the frustration I hold when it comes to constantly having to be on guard in terms of protecting our kids from online harm... unwanted contact from god knows who, brain washing misinformation, the wholly false picture of reality created in developing brains by b*llsh*t content, and then there's online bullying from kids they actually know but can remain under the cloak of anonymity. I'm in danger of sounding ancient, but I when I faced a pretty toxic level of bullying at school, the torment ended when I left the school gates. Now, it's mobile, anonymous, and can be 24/7!

Given the choice, my daughter would literally spend all day in her room on TikTok and Snapchat and my son would be more than happy gluing himself to the PC screen watching endless mind-numbing YouTube videos. We do our best as parents to pull them away from screens, trying to avoid the teenage rebellion that can come with a hardline 'No!'. But the increasing sophistication and addictive draw of the social media algorithms is making it increasingly difficult for parents like us. We all know that asking your kids to leave their phone at home to head out for some family time without distractions runs the risk of starting World War 3. My wife and I are firm on the odd occasion, knowing that life on the screen does nothing but detract from reality of life and hinders the development of simple, yet essential life survival skills... like managing a challenging in-person discussion. Thankfully, my kids, especially my daughter, are growing up to understand the value of opinion, knowing that disagreement is okay, as long as it's dealt with in an agreeable manner.

In its infancy one of the founding social media platforms, Facebook, was a beneficial tool for humankind, providing a digital platform to share **real life** stories and reconnect with old acquaintances regardless of where they reside in the world. It didn't take long for the **'friend'** foundations of the social media business model in the early days to shift to a **'follower'** model (Twitter/X), followed more recently to a **'customer'** led strategy (Instagram). The benefits of connection have been replaced with an increasingly fictitious depiction of life and bodies that kids are being aspired to replicate. And then there's seemingly genuine people earning a decent 'wedge' to persuade people to buy utter sh*t in a bid to reach the fictitious, airbrushed state of self-actualisation they've apparently achieved.

Kids are developing creatures, making them extremely vulnerable. Social media companies, and the influencers they 'platform' are taking full advantage of this! Without strong parenting, constantly using the imaginary eyes in the back of our heads, there's a real danger that feelings of inadequacy will grow at an early age when compared to the online perfection pushed down their throats. And then there's the false picture of reality which is without doubt creating a generation who believe that gratification is instant, life is a breeze, and material possessions are worth more than love, friendship, and solid personal values. I'm genuinely concerned about the potential consequences to the mind health of the generation Z's and Alpha's (and our economy) when they hit their 20's and 30's and face the reality of life, which hasn't changed for centuries... it's f**cking tough and totally unpredictable!

Shocks (in the 'twenties')

Reverting back to Mo Farah's victory in 2012, distinct parallels can be drawn between that final 100 metre sprint and the rapid pace of change that humankind has had no choice but to cope with ever since an uninvited Covid-19 turned up on our shores.

For many, especially those across the western world, accustomed to a life of instant gratification and forgetting the importance of a healthy mind, it's hardly surprising that chaos has ensued since 2020. Covid doused an already burning anxiety epidemic with an oil refinery worth of fuel!

Our grandparents and great grandparents endured significant periods of hardship, restrictions on their freedom and loss of life in numbers that we've never had to experience. I guess this is explains that whilst my then 96-year-old gran expressed concern when the pandemic first hit, I could tell that she wondered what all the fuss was about when it came to the debate about the heavily restricted freedoms imposed by the lockdowns. Having lived through the aftermath of World War 1, through World War 2, the cold war, and the economic turmoil in the 1970's, Covid-19 was just another challenge of many that her generation simply had to get through with a stiff upper lip.

For the majority of under 50's living in the western world, we've only ever witnessed trauma and upheaval in other parts of the world on a screen from the warmth and comfort of our living rooms, images swiftly moving to the back of our minds as the smartphone signals a social media alert. The pandemic, subsequent economic crisis, and the risk of wars in Ukraine and Gaza escalating to a world stage is the first time we've encountered this level of turmoil.

The pandemic created a perfect anxiety storm, that swept across the planet like one of those Texan super-tornadoes, indiscriminate in its choice of which property to raise to the ground and those to bypass. Whether we agree or not with government policies adopted during the height of the pandemic, it's clear that many decisions had an unintentional multiplying effect on the size of the pre-pandemic mental health challenge.

I've got great sadness for the tragic loss of life during the height of the pandemic, but in many respects, the overnight re-engineering of thousands of years of carefully constructed human DNA was significantly more destructive, now carrying long lasting effects. The first UK lockdown remains widely regarded as being the right decision to have been made from all sides, but the stop-start nature of government decisions from there on, varied by postcode, proved catastrophic for our mental stability. Starving the whole of society from essential in-person human contact for such long periods, limiting our interaction with the outside world to a solitary weekly trip to Sainsburys and Saturday night zoom quiz, was never going to end well. The UK was guided through the pandemic like pushing a wonky shopping trolley through the supermarket!

As I write, a little over two years on from the final UK lockdown in 2021, the ripple effect from our response to Covid-19 continues to hit society now, akin to a series of aftershocks following a devastating earthquake:

1. The cost-of-living crisis that emerged and currently running riot through just about every UK household, is having catastrophic consequences for millions, both financially and mentally. Honest, hard-working people have found themselves a position where they are genuinely having to decide between heating their homes or feeding their families, and in extreme cases unable to do either. Whilst the war in Ukraine/Gaza alongside other factors (see later) have clearly compounded our economic instability, the true catalyst was born out of the decision to shut down a finely balanced eco-system that is the 'world economy' multiple times. Don't let any politician or media outlet persuade you otherwise!

I'm an accountant, not an economist, but carry a sufficient level of common sense that tells me that you can't simultaneously pump billions worth of fake money into the system ('quantitive easing') and close down what has become a finely tuned ecosystem of a world economy, only to partially open it and close it multiple times, without serious consequences down the line! It's no f*cking wonder we're living in a cost-of-living crisis (otherwise known as inflation) when monopoly money enters the system and global supply chains are cut.

Despite hindsight now telling us that key aspects of the UK pandemic management strategy we're at best questionable, lockdowns continued to be used beyond 2021 as the primary means to manage Covid-19 by other world governments (e.g. China). This has done nothing but further damage a stalling world economy in desperate need of recovery and starve communities of vital human interaction.

2. I'm not sure if I'll ever come to terms with how we stood by and watched our kids let down so badly during the pandemic. Education was cancelled overnight leaving hard-working parents playing Russian roulette between desperately trying to maintain their job security by keeping the (work) boss extra happy or support their kid's academic development. The government continues to maintain that it's working hard to recover lost teaching ground for what could end up being a forgotten generation, but I'm yet to see any evidence of a structured plan being executed. My concern for the current generation of youth runs wide and deep but remains greatest for the youngest age group during the pandemic who were criminally starved of vital early years social development.

And then there's the way our government targeted children with guilt driven propaganda, that cruelly left them feeling like a 'grim reaper' generation, presenting more danger to society than anyone else. Quotes like "don't kill your gran" (Matt

Hancock, Sept 2020) left kids, especially the youngest, fearful of coming within 2 metres of someone over the age of 60. I mean, how was it expected that kids of primary school age would be able to process a message that they could end up being responsible for the death of a grandparent? F*cking disgraceful at all levels!

3. The right to speak freely (within reason of course) has historically been a cornerstone of British democracy... we disagree, we debate, agree to disagree, then we catch up over a cup of tea or a couple of pints. There have always been boundaries dividing opinion, most notably that between the left and right on our political spectrum. But overall, the 'social contract' that until recently sat at the heart of British culture has always engendered a level of mutual respect where opinions differ.

Arguably Brexit was the first time we've seen dividing lines of opinion harden to the point that all sense of toleration went out of the window. I was one of many who voted to leave the EU back in 2016 and then swiftly moved on in my life... the exception being anorexia which nearly destroyed me. 7 years on from the referendum and despite a rare case of political alignment between the Tories and Labour to crack on, the Brexit battleground continues to thrive. A classic example would be Robert Peston's 'WTF' which I now regret ever deciding to read. Whilst it was well written piece of literature (far better than what you're reading now), it did nothing more than to try and convince the reader that the UK would sink into 3rd world status following the democratic decision to leave the EU. Bo**cks! Brexit created noticeable step towards dividing our once broadly balanced society, but when Covid-19 arrived on British shores and spread like wildfire, it the problem became far worse. If you so much as muttered even a healthy level of skepticism about the government mandated lockdowns or mask wearing, you'd be shut down immediately. Those of us with an inquisitive and questioning nature but carrying a positive intent (like me!), found ourselves forever in a position where we were forced to gently tease out the view of others to establish if we were safe enough to express a perfectly balanced opinion.

Social media became and has remained a battle ground to this day, with wars being fought across numerous issues… between who I refer to as the 'indoctrinated' and people who for genuine and balanced reasons don't prescribe to what we're supposedly meant to think. Yes, there will always be hardline w*nkers out there, but I genuinely believe they are in the minority. Feeling brave enough to publicly question the 'script' and you run the risk of becoming a social leper, and in extreme cases can even put your livelihood and family's security at risk.

We can't remain mentally fit and well if we live in fear of expressing our opinions or left carrying guilt simply because we carry a different stance to the mainstream!

Some people did arrive at the other side of the pandemic relatively unscathed, but in my very humble opinion, the difference between succumbing to mental ill-health or riding the storm relatively unscathed, was largely down to personal circumstance. I can't begin to think what it must have been like for a self-employed single parent with young children living in isolation facing a very real decision between supporting their children's education or having leave them at home to earn a wage. This is the type of stuff that is rarely talked about!

Silenced

"Just because you're offended doesn't mean you're right"

Ricky Gervais

*"Being offended on behalf of someone else is b*llshit. It's virtue signalling and it's condescending"*

Jimmy Carr
(Before & Laughter)

I'm in danger of painting a siloed mentality of myself by revisiting the topic of (restricted) free speech. But the scale of the issue and harm it's causing warrants an attempt to unpack the challenge in more detail.

In truth, I've found this specific section of the book the hardest to write by a country mile. I've typed, deleted, and re-typed it countless times. Why? Because like so many others, I fear the prospect of being 'cancelled' just for daring to touch on subjects where debate has largely been paralysed through risk of causing offense. The very fact I've pluck up the courage to share what I believe to be a set of well-balanced personal opinions is in itself a pretty sorry state of affairs.

What's even more saddening is the overwhelming urge sat at the centre of my gut to start by outwardly stating that I genuinely believe in a society based on freedom and equality (i.e., I'm not a bad guy!). I've never judged anyone on the basis of their ethnicity, gender, or socio-economic background… in fact, anything that makes someone different to me. The urge to justify oneself as a decent human being before simply voicing thought through opinions is a fundamental issue that is now crippling society. This growing feature of modern-day Britain is doing nothing more than tightening the lid on perfectly natural feelings and genuine opinions that carry no founding malice. In my humble opinion, continuing to suppress the freedom of constructive expression through fear of ill-founded character judgement cannot co-exist with a healthy mind.

More controversial subject matters have always existed, but in the past, sound minded people were able to debate in an agreeable manner, starting with differing views and usually open to the idea that someone else could change their stance. The freedom to discuss, debate and ultimately educate each other without fear of being shut down or 'cancelled' is exactly how 'taboo' subjects (at a point in time) have now become normalised in everyday society. Right now, I see the freedom of debate being tested to breaking point as the everyday man, woman and child are seemingly being indoctrinated to think and live life in a certain way. Fail to tow the line, or simply ask perfectly reasoned questions, and you run the risk of being judged as a hate figure, absent of empathy, or simply a bigot. We have an increasingly diverse society, which I see as nothing but a positive thing. But this in some respects this been achieved at the expense of our diversity in opinion.

Ever heard of Dr Jordan Peterson? I hadn't until I stumbled across a Piers Morgan interview, with Peterson's responses to Morgan's questions making an instant and strong connection. Peterson, a Canadian clinical psychologist and all-round 'free thinker', has a vast intellect that has left me struggling to comprehend many of his philosophical points when I manage to dip into his podcasts that I've recently started listening to. Owing to his outspoken critical (and in my opinion balanced) assessment of subjects that modern society deem as 'no go' areas, he's become a leading voice for a growing number of people. During that first encounter with Peterson, Morgan asked him what at the time I thought to be an odd question… "what is the biggest threat to mankind?". His response was far from expected, yet incredibly simple, powerful, and thought provoking. Rather than the usual suspects you'd expect in a response… the destruction of humankind from the force of global warming, the increasing sophistication of AI leading to scenes similar to those depicted by the 1980s film 'Terminator', or the risk of current (2023) conflicts in Ukraine and Gaza / tension in Taiwan Strait escalating to a world level…. the response was… **"narcissistic compassion".**

Narcissistic Compassion

"The compassionate narcissist would look like they are protecting someone or look like they're protecting a religion, a culture, a race, a belief, a gender, often by attacking the very

people who don't, then playing the woe is me victim who's been attacked when the very people they're attacking call them out, with claims such as "I'm only trying to help." Or "it's only because I care.""

Elizabeth Shaw (Blogger)

I actually prefer:

"The momentum driven by sections of the mainstream media, education system, sporting bodies, political parties, and in cases the companies we work for, to alter our already learnt thinking and behaviours simply to align to a an ever-shifting pre-conditioned script. Failure to stick to the script when outside of your trusted circle, even if when articulating an opinion backed up by a well-reasoned rationale, you run the risk (at best) of becoming a social/professional outcast or face the prospect (at worst) of being 'cancelled' altogether."

Me

The direction of travel in recent years has become increasingly binary and, in many respects, highly politicised. At times it feels (to me) like that the entire middle ground of debate has evaporated into thin air, replaced by a polarised and in my opinion, left leaning thinking which blocks everything else, even those only marginally right of centre.

I see society slowly being forced to adopt ways of thinking through guilt driven propaganda through mainstream and social media platforms and even the school curriculum, aimed at shutting down the politically right views (even a couple of steps right of centre). How?... by generating fear…

1. You hold genuine, reasoned concerns about the drain on already depleted and failing social services, not to mention the unknown risk to our national security, from increasing levels of illegal immigration. You ask yourself why the government is spending millions every day on accommodation for migrants who enter the country illegally when the poorest in society are struggling to heat their homes and/or put food on the table and we allow British people to live on the streets = you lack empathy for their plight, or worse still, you're a racist… **TOTALLY AND UTTERLY WRONG!**

2. We can't 'Just Stop Oil' overnight in a global economy that remains overwhelmingly powered by fossil fuels. Equally, despite Britain's past, when the impact from industrialisation could not be foreseen, the UK which now omits less than 1% of the world's carbon emissions, should not take the brunt of the burden when this comes with an immediate and sizeable price tag that ultimately drives the poorest in society into deeper levels of poverty = you're a climate change denier or have no regard for future of your children and grandchildren… **WRONG!**

The spectrum of irony in the whole climate change debate is broad and far reaching, mainly because the facts we're given from both sides of the argument never actually speak the same language. This makes it impossible for the 'average Jo' like me to differentiate solid scientific fact from utter cobblers. My personal approach is to adopt a more simplistic stance… if you ask anyone on the street if they want to live on a cleaner planet and you can guarantee the answer will be a resounding "yes". Ask them the same underlying question but this time add that achieving this goal will come with a big price tag when they're already living on the breadline, and throw in additional context that both China and India are building countless new coal fire stations, adding to the 40% of world carbon they already omit… I strongly suspect this would generate a range of different responses. The simple fact is the public are crying out for one version of the truth on this high-profile subject versus the barrage of hate (evidenced on Twitter/X) and conflicting statistics we're plied with from both sides of the debate.

3. When you look back through British History history, whilst you'd never consider the thought of supporting the ills of the British Empire's past through the lens of of modern-day society, you don't feel guilt for the actions of our now disconnected forefathers and consider it fundamentally wrong that we should erase elements of our past = you celebrate the wrongs of our colonial past... **WRONG!**

4. You are a very genuine supporter of the vision to create a more equitable landscape across both gender and racial diversity in the workplace. As the same time, you ponder over whether the pendulum has swung too quickly, with some corporate business's inadvertently harming their short to medium term commercial prospects in favour of scoring 'inclusivity' points in a bid to build marketing collateral. Bringing to life the genuine benefits you'd expect from a skilled, diverse workplace without the risk of diluting the competitiveness from market leading expertise will not take decades to achieve. But it can't be achieved overnight, so needs a more rational, patient, and structured societal approach supported by all corners including responsible parenting and improved core education = you favour the white British male remaining professionally dominant... **FUNDAMENTALLY WRONG!**

I fully recognise that I'm about to step into dangerous territory, but I can't address the subject of free speech without reflecting on the highly publicised debate that's emerged on the subject of transgender rights. In my opinion this debate has now surpassed both Brexit and the pandemic when it comes the accompanying level of toxicity.

Stepping into this very delicate space, the only place I can start is with J.K Rowling. When it comes to Rowling's work, I'm the first to admit that I'm no fan, in fact I'm firmly sat in the minority having shown no interest in the Harry Potter books or spin off films (i.e., I'm tackling this thorny subject with complete objectivity!).

Back in 2020, Rowling took to Twitter/X, tweeting the following:

> *"'People who menstruate.' I'm sure there used to be a word for those people. Someone help me out. Wumben? Wimpund? Woomud?"*

When I first read Rowling's tweet, my initial reaction was to think that it was nothing more than a candid response with a touch of sarcastic humour in response to an article she'd attached. The article, published by Devex, focused on the impact of the pandemic in terms of restricted access to essential female hygiene products in parts of the world. Rowling's response showed no sign of any disagreement with the over-arching theme of the article but pointed towards a clear deep and underlying concern that Devex replaced one word ('women') with 'people'. I'm no expert but I think I'm educated enough to understand that whilst a tiny minority of non-binary people can/do menstruate, the vast majority of those who do are actually women.

As an accountant I tend to approach life on a basis of fact. With this in mind I'd say that Rowling made nothing more than a perfectly acceptable point. If you re-read her words with cold objectivity and no prior knowledge of situation that would ultimately follow, I'd say they weren't in the slightest bit offensive, nor did they point to an underlying hate towards the transgender community. My rather simple interpretation is that she was merely exercising her right to constructive free speech by expressing her implied opinion that as one of >50% of the world's population herself, she considered the wording used in the Devex article represented an erosion of her female identity.

Personally, and maybe this is because I do take a blunt and factually based stance, I'd say that someone of Rowling's stature whose opinion was always going to carry far, was merely using her stature to voice words of solidarity across her millions of female followers. But the reality of the response from large parts of the online community, swiftly followed by the mainstream media, was very different to my take on the situation. Twitter execs sat back; arms crossed, smoking gigantic Havana cigars as the ad driven neon dollar signs lit up from a tidal wave of online hate pointed towards Rowling. They did nothing more than observe Rowling being hunted online under the cloak of online anonymity, which included some pretty sickening threats of rape and even murder.

It's an entirely valid perception that since that post in 2020, Rowling has gone on to antagonise hard line transactivists with a regular flurry of Twitter posts. But has her entrenched stance been down a genuine transphobic mindset, or is it be down to the fact she's strong and ultimately wealthy enough stand by her right to express her opinion without fear of a life changing impact to her financial security? Personally, I'd say it's probably the latter.

So, where has Rowling's experience left other like-minded women who may want to express similar shared concerns? The simple answer is **'silenced'**, petrified of facing similar retribution. Even politicians have shied away from what's arguably now become a fully loaded question from sections of the media, "can you define a woman?". Countless MPs, including the current leader of His Majesty's opposition (which could change in 2024) have curled up into a foetal position, petrified of losing votes at the next general election if he were to go as far as respond to the question by simply reciting the dictionary definition, "an adult female human being". The only people brave enough to challenge without fear are those in parts of the mainstream media who earn a living from calling out this type of madness… i.e., they get paid to say the things that many are thinking but simply too afraid to say.

Like every other human being, I'm far from immune to personal faults but on balance consider myself to be a person of good character. With this comes a firm opinion that everyone should be able to live alongside each other despite their differences and without fear of discrimination. But I also believe that harmony cannot be achieved simply by forcing ways of thinking on people. When it comes to transgender rights, yes, there will be sick extremists out there who take an unacceptable hardline stance against this minority group, but I firmly believe they also sat in a minority group. But what about those who carry genuine personal concerns about some of the things they see or simply have a knowledge gap they're happy to be filled? One thing's for sure, they shouldn't be muted from asking questions or constructively challenging the narrative, even if executed with a slice of sarcasm.

I've got two kids, and to be perfectly frank, I honestly don't give a "you know what" however they decide to identify… but only when they've worked it out for themselves! All I care about is that my kids grow through life guided by the values their parents have tried to install in them, in the hope that whilst they will end up imperfect (like all of us), they end up as all-round good people in society.

Alongside solid parenting, the education system has a big role to play in teaching our kids to respect differences in society. However, in my humble opinion and that of other parents I've mustered the courage to share my concerns with, kids, some of primary school age, are being exposed to the elements of gender ideology way too early in life. This must be leaving them feeling them confused and sometimes pressurised by the education system to think and identify in an adult way before they've had sufficient time to work who they are and what they want to be. Maybe it's my 'conservative' mindset that hinders my ability to think progressively, but I can't help but stand by the principle that the education system is there to teach our kids to respect differences, not sell them the concept of choosing between one of 70+ gender identities. My view is that as guardians of our children, parents been left totally in the dark, frustrated, and angry in cases, by the absence of any consultation from the education system (that we pay for) to ratify that including this teaching in the curriculum is something **we want** for our kids. As the same time, we feel powerless to voice our concerns, knowing it's more than likely to result in accusations of transphobia.

It's this type of genuine, non-hateful concern that I should be allowed to express without any fear of retribution, knowing I'm entirely open to a have my concern alleviated (or reinforced) if I'm given the chance to debate in a respectful manner. It's this open and honest debate that society is now desperately missing.

My concern on this specific topic goes beyond the curricula world, extending to the distinct lack of perspective we're witnessing in legislation, which in my very simple mind increases the risk of women coming into harm's way. Please note my careful choice of words… 'increase in risk'… I **didn't** point to a 'guaranteed' risk. When it comes to legislation like Scotland's Gender Reform Bill, there's also little acknowledgement that it runs the distinct risk of actually fueling discontent towards the trans community, serving to divide society rather than make it more inclusive. Whilst I don't agree with this type of legislation, I'm mature enough not to allow the actions of legislative authorities create a bias towards trans people. At the same time, the reality is that equality has never been achieved by (rightly or wrongly) being seen to alienate the majority.

The vile online rhetoric that's now become a normalised form of ammunition to shut people down the moment they speak up, runs the risk of leaving others incapable of fulfilling their human right of expression or even worse feeling a sense of self-loathing for simply having a different view to the narrative of the day. This cadged mentality, which I truly believe is more common that recognised, can easily play into the hands of mental ill-health, and from there, an admittedly unquantifiable risk of mapping a path to self-harming ways of coping.

More recently, the better segments of our media have started to expose the growing problem of 'Social Cancellation', headlined by the story surrounding the decision by Coutts, a bank for the wealthy, to close Nigel Farage's bank account. Only after Farage filed a subject access request was it revealed the bank's decision was down to nothing more than his political views. I'm pretty agnostic when it comes Farage but it's fair to say he's a divisive character and someone who some would see as the most influential person in politics never to be elected as a member of parliament. That aside, the incident with Coutts exposed a bigger and deeply concerning issue where simply having the courage to challenge elements of the accepted wisdom of the day is being used by financial institutions under the guise of ESG (Environmental, Social & Governance) target to deny tens of thousands of UK citizens from access to fundamental human right… money!

I genuinely fear for the future balance of our society if parts, quite possibly the majority (?), if they continue to be silenced on complex subjects like gender identity, illegal immigration, and climate change. Thankfully, now in my 40's, I mature and level-headed enough to ride the storm (aside from this rant). But there is a distinct and very real risk that shutting down debate will only lead to the more susceptible members of society who feel gagged, being drawn to more extremist viewpoints. We should all have our eyes wide open to this risk in the knowledge that history tells us that creating hard line divisions in society never ends well!

"Changing minds isn't about attacking people's views. It starts with seeking to understand their views."

Adam Grant

Snowflake Society

"Criticising "woke culture" has become a way of claiming victim status for yourself rather than acknowledging that more deserving others hold that status."

The Guardian (2020)

The quote above, taken from an article published in the Guardian, goes a long way to support Dr Jordan Peterson's powerful words citing "narcissistic compassion" as the number one threat facing the world today. The underlying message is loud and clear…disagree with any element of the vast spectrum of beliefs that form woke ideology = you're a low life and inept of any level of human empathy. What utter bo**ocks!

There are different schools of thought about when 'woke' thinking was first born. Some argue that it dates back to the 1940s, when it was considered a 'progressive' way of thinking. But it entered the US mainstream at the start of the Black Lives Matter movement in the early noughties. Like all things American, it wasn't long before the UK caught the US virus, with this illness leaving an admittedly imperfect, but on the whole inclusive British culture, bed bound until further notice.

As I suspect you've already gathered, I'm no fan of the woke led thinking, but I'm in total ore of how what I view as religious style cult has drawn in those on the 'left' into some kind of hypnotic trance, wearing the ideology like a badge that distinguishes good from bad. Of course, we should seek ways and means to think and act more progressively, helping to iron out the creases that remain in modern day Britain, but it cannot be at the expense of destroying the foundations that for centuries have distinguished one national identity from another. It's farcical that in a progressive bid to create greater diversity the western world is seemingly trying to form a single monoculture, leaving what were once independent national cultures increasingly indistinguishable from one another.

The culture war we now find ourselves in runs deep across all parts of society. Both public and private sector organisations are at war with each other, trying to 'out-woke' opponents in their respective fields in an attempt to score valuable brownie points from the metropolitan elite… those in the wealthy suburbs of London who have little to absolutely no idea about what real life is like for the average British man or women. What both public and private sectors haven't cottoned onto is that vast numbers of us aren't stupid and can see right through the utter hypocrisy that often materialises from the virtue signalling rhetoric we see spouted on a daily basis.

In the large corporate sector, the rush to enhance brand value with a woke affiliation is now starting to backfire on businesses. Why? Because it doesn't take much for a brand connection with woke ideology to conflict with the very principle of capitalist enterprise… to maximise shareholder wealth! Take Unilever as a case in point. This consumer brand giant has increasingly signalled its virtue over the last decade, possibly in bid to capitalise on the growing consumer trend to buy based on ethical stance rather than good old price point. A classic example from Unilever was the withdrawal of Ben and Jerry's ice cream from sale in Israeli occupied Palestinian territory. Personally, I don't have a stance on politics surrounding this decision, but where I do have a problem is that following the country's invasion of sovereign Ukraine, Unilever continued to sell their products in Russia. If you publicly set your stall out to protest against an invasion of sovereignty, you stick to the principle. The fact is, and we all know it, when it comes down to it, money talks, and always will in the capitalist world we live in!

Editing note: *My reference to Israel/Palestine is by no means an attempt to make a political point. This was written a before the start of the 2023 conflict. Like everyone, I've got my views on the subject, but thought best to stay quiet rather than risk being 'silenced' by the public court of opinion!*

Shareholders in businesses like Unilever, particularly the big institutional investors, demand a high yield on the capital they invest. Maybe I'm cynical, but do you think the reported £500 million per annum Unilever makes from the Russian market could have been the reason why they didn't follow the likes of MacDonalds (a business I never thought I'd call out for its moral standing), by exiting the Russian market? I'm not suggesting the commercial decision was the wrong to make, but I do find the hypocrisy infuriating.

The hypocrisy I see across the woke a elite bl**dy annoying, especially when it comes from the king of woke himself, Gary Linekar. I'd be pretty f*cking stupid to try and to connect the rise of this culture with the deterioration in societal mental health seen over recent years. But where I firmly believe woke thinking has had an impact on mental health, especially in men, is what I can only describe as an ideological march to remove all forms of fun from life…unless of course you're one of those living in Islington (North London) who get an overwhelming fortnightly stimulus from the prospect of wheeling out an overflowing recycling bin, smug in the acknowledgement that yet again you've outdone your next door neighbour in the battle to save the planet!

I've absolutely no data to evidence my hypothesis, so I'm going to have to just gamble by calling it out… the direction of travel seemingly aimed at making our daily way of life as 'wet' as possible is making us miserable, especially across British men who are feeling more and more alienated. Elements of the hard line woke community will love reading these words, possibly viewing it as a 'mission accomplished' moment. Afterall, aren't men, especially white men, to blame for all the wrongs in the world? Granted, a tiny percentage of powerful and predominantly white men are probably accountable for reinforcing/building on existing societal inequalities, but blame cannot rest at the door of your 'average Joe'. Despite this the woke brigade seemingly continue to do their best to weaken the foundations across the many of the essential things us 'average Joe's' rely on to keep us sane. We all know that men are basic creatures, relying heavily on escapism as a means to support their wellbeing. Be it the continued threat to harmless banter between **consenting** males in the pub / workplace, or the vast politicisation of the sport they watch, British men are seeing a gradual, consistent erosion of the sanity inducing experiences they rely heavily on, usually in the name of equality.

The list of tangible examples to evidence my point is endless, but one stands out… when the Welsh Rugby Union (RFU) banned 'Delilah' from being played at national games. Welsh blood doesn't run through my veins, but I think I'm pretty safe in my perception that this famous Tom Jones record, first released in the 1960's, comes a close second to "Old Land of My Fathers" as the official Welsh national anthem. Widely considered a track forever connected with good times, sat in the same league as "Common Eileen", the vast majority of people (including myself) have no personal connection with the lyrics, which I now understand is the story of a jealous man who murders his lover. So, what did the Welsh RFU do? They banned it, presumably thinking that whilst stretching their vocal cords singing Delilah, the lyrics would somehow prompt the male fans to return home to their wives as misogynistic beasts. Or was it an attempt to protect female fans from the threat of intimidating lyrics? All I can say is, what a load of complete and utter bo**ocks! Thankfully, following the announcement, common sense prevailed, with the Welsh fans sticking two almighty fingers up at the sporting body by bellowing out Delilah despite the absence of the backing track. The problem here is that we are seeing this type of situation become a normalised common occurrence in daily life. There's a natural tendency to laugh it off when we hear the news on the radio or read what we consider to be a ridiculous story in the newspaper. But we shouldn't underestimate the compound impact of these small yet consistent changes that do nothing but gradually eat away at our identity.

I f*cking hate guys like Andrew Tate, seeing just how dangerous he is, not only to the reputation of mankind, but the risk he presents to a more vulnerable younger generation of boys and men who are far more susceptible to his vile influence. Despite the hate this ar*hole constantly points towards women, he remains platformed on Twitter/X and as of August 2023 had over 7.5 million followers. Of course, a small minority of his followers will be born and bred misogynists, but the vast majority won't be when they first show an interest in what he's got to say. I strongly suspect that the majority of his follows are made up of disillusioned men who feel consistently put down and 'de-maled' by parts of society, purely on the grounds of their sex. Having a teenage daughter myself, I'm genuinely concerned about the potential impact on the safety of women from the growing level of discontent in young men who end up finding solace in the vile rhetoric spouted by the likes of Tate. All I can say is that on this particular point I genuinely hope that I'm wrong.

Still, there may be a glimmer of hope:

> *"There's only so woke and liberal you can get and then you start going the other way. But it's inevitable."*
>
> *Ricky Gervais (2021)*

Maybe Gervais' statement was a premonition, illustrated more recently by Nicola Sturgeon's high-profile resignation as the first minister of Scotland after twisting herself in knots having embraced the woke agenda into the bosom of the SNP by refusing to recognise that a convicted trans rapist was actually a man and a danger to women in a women only jail. I think (and hope) that we're finally starting to see the British public stand up to this nonsense, kickstarting the 'great reverse'… finally taking us back to a point of sanity.

If you lean to left of the political spectrum, you may well have finished this section thinking "this guy is f*cking right wing old codger". Whilst my political persuasion does indeed sit right of centre, it's only a couple of steps from the middle, definitely not miles. And yes, I'm at the ripe old age of 44 but not yet approaching deaths door. I'd like to think I've got a few more miles left in the tank before I reach the milestone of 'old codger'. The genuine truth is that I'm really concerned about the direction we're heading in, which rather than creating the intended equal and fairer society, it's actually leaving the majority feeling marginalised.

State Corruption & Incompetence

Our political system has now moved way beyond being a mere source of irritation to the everyday man/woman on the street. As things stand (in 2023), I'd say it's a f*cking write-off! In my opinion this is now the view held by the majority of the UK public, which conflicts with a now vastly outdated, yet ever present cultural perception that Britain, with its unique traditions steeped in pomp and ceremony, is still firmly fixed at the top of the moral high ground. British culture is founded on the perception of a morally superior status that we think is admired from afar, our well-oiled political system with its weird traditions dating back to the 13th century being the foundation to justify this status.

The British voter was immunised long ago from the liberalised truth used by Politicians whodo noting but sidestep questions with obscure bullsh*t, failing to deliver a f*cking straight "yes" or "no". In itself this has always been a point of frustration but on the whole an accepted pain in the ar*e by the electorate.

But, over the last decade the low-level smoke and mirrors we're accustomed to have hit a whole new level from both sides of the political spectrum. This issue has been compounded by the increasingly complex data driven world we live in, making it far too easy to manipulate outcomes, leaving the difference between right and wrong impossible to decipher. But the thing that has riled me more than anything else are the ever more frequent instances of political corruption that test all levels of morality… plus the sheer f*cking incompetence we've seen from both political chambers over recent years. This have left far more than a just the bitter taste of unfairness in the mouth across vast swads of the British electorate!

I've held a keen interest in the British political landscape ever since making the unfashionable decision to study A Level Politics. Until the 2018 general election I remained firm in the view that in spite of the odd scandal…as a Chelsea fan, David Mellor's run-in with the 'red tops' in the 90's always springs to mind (if you're under 45, look it up!) … our political system is one of the most reputable in western society, and a personal decision not to cast your vote means you waive any right to complain. But it's taken less than a single year parliamentary term for me and countless others to become so disillusioned with our so-called democratic system, that I'm likely to opt for a spoilt ballet paper at the next general election. I know this type of pettiness will carry no chance of deriving any form of 'Citizen Smith' outcome, but I envisage the distinct sense of relief (albeit temporary) this action would give me. My spoilt ballot would contain words along the lines of the following:

"This country including with the hearts and minds of millions of voters is now on its knees, largely due to the egotistical mismanagement by the utter w**kers we've entrusted to run it. Until our political system reverts to one founded on serving the interests of the electorate rather than itself, you can take my democratic right and shove it firmly up you're a*se… sideways!"

What politicians haven't yet woken up to is the impact from the normalisation of Westminster scandals. MPs from all sides consistently take the p*ss out of the electorate through a combination of extreme levels of self-indulgency and power-hungry tactics. Political scandals are now so frequent that they are no longer classified as such, with the very real impact from mismanagement on the daily life of average voters literally screwing with their minds. Queue the age-old response; "it's always been like this". But has it always been this bad?

The list of scandals we've witnessed over recent years have been shocking and endless in numbers... millions wasted on dodgy PPE contracts, illegal lockdown parties, £140m given to Rwanda with absolutely no contractual recourse when unsurprisingly the 'Mickey Mouse' immigration policy is destined to collapse, peerages given to countless members of the 'old boys' club.... And the most infuriating scandal of all... Matt f*cking Hancock himself!... Once the Health Secretary who clearly got a perverse kick out of the grip he held over the British public during the pandemic (just read the WhatsApp messages leaked to the Daily Telegraph), who turned into a wet little boy in the jungle (or boy who wet himself), only to pop up in a 'Led by Donkeys' sting operation quoting his daily consultancy rate at a whopping £10k a day (look it up). The fact that our state system would continue to allow this egotistical, corrupt w**ker (my opinion) to continue walking the halls of Westminster (in 2023), only goes to incapsulate the problem. Given half a chance I'd have forced fed him raw camel sh*t when he appeared on I'm a Celebrity Get me out of Here!

The fact is, while a small minority of genuinely good MPs do exist, following the accepted principle of working to serve the interest of their constituents, the majority of MPs (in my opinion) are there to serve a single interest... their own career progression. These are the 'political elite' who enter politics with zero, if any, experience of living in the real world. Just to be clear, referencing "the real world" doesn't mean a pre political life working for an investment bank after 'daddy' negotiated a career opening when he hit a triple-bogey on 18th hole to lose a round of golf with the CEO! This out of touch culture that spans the halls Westminster has left us with at best, average talent across the chamber elected to run our country. Parallels can indeed be drawn between Westminster and the private sector (privilege tends to take you places) but I'd say 80% of the 650 current elected MPs would be escorted from the premises of a corporate business hugging their box of belongings way before the end of their probationary period!

What happens in parliament if you're performance is below par? You get to stay in the job for 5 years (in most instances), the exceptions being a demotion to the back benches or having the party whip withdrawn. There's little to no risk of MPs losing their job, no matter how sh*t they are at the job! Then, when they eventually leave their seat in the Commons, they depart with a final salary state pension!

Liz Truss' tenure as Prime Minister brings my point to life… outlasted by the shelf-life of a f*cking lettuce and modelled her tenure on the 1960's cartoon series 'Batfink'. Alongside her crimefighting partner Kamikaze Kwarteng (aka 'Karate'), she tanked the UK economy overnight with a fiscal strategy straight out of pre-school. I actually agreed with many the underlying principles in what these two bozos were trying to do, but to announce such radical changes in that 'mini budget' with little to no socialisation/validation with the financial markets was a f*cking crime in itself! Having served for a mere 45 days, she's entitled to a £115,000 annual state pension. It literally makes me want to throw up!

The everyday person, who works their a*rse off day in day out, sometimes seven days a week across multiple jobs, that's left with nothing left after necessities have been covered, hasn't just become disconnected from British politics. They've been left financially and mentally scared from what the political elite have done to their lives through the utter mismanagement of our country over the years. I'm actually starting to sound like Mick Lynch rather than a consistent Tory voter…that is, until now!

As I type I can see the Labour voters among you rubbing your hands with glee having just read my damming attack on the pre 2024 election Tory government. Afterall "we cannot get any worse than a bunch of scum, homophobic, racist, misogynistic, absolute vile … banana republic, vile, nasty, Etonian … piece of scum" (Angela Raynor's take on 13 years of Tory government). But the fact is, whatever spin Labour may put on it, his majesty's official opposition have been about as effective as their internal governance that allowed an antisemitic virus to spread through its rank and file!

Whether we like it or not, in a system based on career politics, our democratically elected infrastructure does little more than support a continuation of incompetent management across everything the government extracts our hard-earned taxes to pay for. Unlike the 1980's when both Tories and Labour were fuelled but genuine political ideologies miles apart from each other, they've now merged into one of the same thing… sat within immediate reach of each other on the ideological spectrum, with little to no substance but plenty of sound bites. As we currently head towards a general election in 2024, hard line Labour supporters will disagree with my point of view … an opinion they're wholly entitled to. The proof will be in the pudding if Labour do win the election in 2024, but for now, if I hear Kier Starmer, "captain flip-flop" himself, mutter the words "sticky plaster politics" one more time, I swear that I'm going to have a big and very embarrassing public meltdown. Before I step off my political soapbox ("thank god for that"… your words, not mine!), I can't help but share with my own thoughts on a couple of the key changes I'd say would go a little way to address the issues I've rather vocally ranted about:

1. One blatantly obvious change would be to introduce a framework across the halls of Westminster akin to the type of tight Human Resource policy and control structure we see in large corporate businesses. Why?

Firstly, there's currently little to no deterrent in place to stop a continued influx of scandals that will only go to further discredit an already marred reputation across both elected and unelected political chambers. I mean, for heaven's sake, during the current parliamentary term, which thankfully will end in 2024, we've seen resignations and even prison terms handed out for offences, including an MP watching porn videos in the house of commons, a sickening historical sexual assault on a minor, raping a spouse, unwanted sexual advances (including groping), and referring to a female political aid as "sugar t*ts". Has the seemingly obvious concept of collating independent character references and coordinating background checks ever been considered? Afterall, would a 'referee' risk the damage to their own reputation if they provide a glowing reference for an electoral candidate when they've personally witnessed vile misogynistic behaviors from them in the past. This is exactly what happens in the private sector when recruiting for positions of trust, where a simple 'decline to provide' on request for a character reference will speak volumes for the hiring business.

Secondly, once a serious wrongdoing is exposed and confirmed, you'd think the steps to oust an MP from their parliamentary seat would be straightforward and quick. In which case, you'd be wrong! Parliament is seemingly able to respond in the same way as a private sector employer (i.e. employment contract ripped up with an immediate dismissal). Yes, MPs can lose the party whip, effectively leaving them as a political nomad, but they retain their seat in the House and continue to earn a salary. In the current parliamentary term we've seen this happen to the likes of Dianne Abbot and Jeremy Corbin, both able to continue sitting as independents despite having publicly displayed themselves as antisemites (in my opinion). The case of Margaret Ferrier illustrates just how hard it is to oust an MP who clearly lacks a morale conscience. The SNP MP broke the law back in 2020 by taking a train from Scotland to Westminster, despite having tested positive for Covid-19. Despite having had the whip removed by the SNP and being ordered to serve 270 hours of community service, she defiantly refused to resign. That was until three years later, when a 30-day parliamentary suspension finally allowed her own constituents to kick her out, forcing a by-election. How the f*ck can this feel right in any sense of the imagination?

2. By far and away the change we can make to stem the flow of the spiraling damage being caused by the halls of Westminster would be a shift away from our current electoral system, 'First Past the Post' (FPTP)… to Proportional Representation (PR). I know, I know, I'm sounding like a bl**dy Lib Dem rather than a traditional Conservative! Put simply, if we can't rely on the two-party system served up by FPTP to serve in the interests of the British electorate (rather than themselves), the obvious solution to install the accountability the electorate craves is move to a system that rewards representation in the main political chamber in proportion with the way we vote.

Until more recently, my stance on PR has always been a firm 'No', owing to the coalition led governments this system creates. I've always been on the side of the those who argue that coalitions are less decisive which leads to political and economic stagnation. I'm now in a position where the two-party system delivered by FPTP gives the electorate no other choice than between 'sh*t' and 'sh*tter'. Change is needed to finally remove the main two from the comfort zone they've sat in for decades, forcing them to start acting in our interest.

Evidence shows that PR does work to dilute instances of political corruption and forces elected representatives to work harder for the people who provide them with a living. The top 10 countries in the 2022 Corruption Perceptions Index, an annual index run since the mid 90's ranking 180 countries "by their perceived levels of public sector corruption", all use PR as their main electoral system. Unsurprisingly, the United Kingdom has seen its index position slide from 10th in 2000 to 18th in 2022, now sat below the likes of Uruguay… it doesn't instinctively feel like the UK is sat on the pedestal that the establishment would like us to believe we sit on!

Silicon (Valley)

The first five sides of my cuboid have revealed what I refer to as the (potential) **ignitors** of a path towards mental ill-health, which from personal experience is a solitary step away an addiction dominated existence. The final side reveals what is without any doubt the category that adds **fuel** to an addiction flame.

I've touched on the connection our social media driven world and growing societal challenges, but the depth of influence these platforms have on the life necessitates a little more 'unpacking' ….in the context of addiction!

Silicon Valley, the northern area of California and home to the world's mobile tech giants, social media platforms, and global search engines, has without doubt changed the world forever… in some respects, for the better, but in many others for the worse, especially when it comes to the influence they carry by dousing petrol on the addiction flame.
Granted, the monetisation of addiction won't appear in the output of the annual strategic planning cycle of any of the social media giants. But the cutthroat nature of this media sector with the big players all fighting in the same pond of advertising revenue has without doubt created an online world where addicts are actively stalked. When (virtually) hunted by the very things that keep your illness connect to you it becomes virtually impossible to break free from free.

Let me explain…

1. Once hooked, with the victim firmly wedded to the underpinning "musts" that accompany addiction led illnesses, the tendency is to actively seek new ways to strengthen the illusion of an entirely false marriage made in heaven. During my own honeymoon period with anorexia, I quickly became drawn to social media platforms in search for like-minded people… but without the aim of seeking comfort or finding help! Instead, I was looking for new strategies to strengthen the relationship I'd forged with my newly wedded anorexic spouse.

I find it outrageous that social media platforms go beyond the ethical boundaries of free speech by allowing users to promote ways to strengthen an illness. To help illustrate, a simple Twitter/X search for "Anorexia Nervosa" brought up the following as the first return of many promoting the benefits of the illness:

Twitter/X Handle: Anorexiajunkie

Headline: "I want my body to thinner than my sanity"

Followers: 11,000

Latest Post: "Thanks to alcohol for making me puke my guts out last night bc [because] I lost 1.4lbs"

Moving onto Instagram, I ran the same search, but this time I'm presented with a warning indicating the risk of harmful content. The message offers support, should I "be going through a difficult time", which takes the user through to contact numbers for Beat, probably the best-known UK eating disorder charity. Whilst the warning and offer of support are without any doubt positive, an addict living in complete denial that a problem exists will simply ignore the warning and click 'okay to proceed'. So, I do just that, opening up the door to some really disturbing images. The one I still can't get out of my head (for the entirely wrong reasons) was an account held by a girl, who'd I say was no older than 16, maybe younger. Viewing her public account was horrifying, containing a catalogue of images of what can only be described as selfies of her emaciated frame in front of a mirror. From the images, I'd say she couldn't have weighed a single pound over 5 stone, the diameter of her biceps appearing no bigger than a baby's wrist, collar bones so protracted that you could literally hang a coat on them. The images of this clearly mentally and physically unwell girl, quite possibly a minor, were heart-breaking to see. But the thing that made it even more disturbing was that this poor girl had over 17,000 followers! This leads me to beg the question… in our current age of online influencers, could the fame this girl feels from having such a huge following actually be reinforcing a path to destruction?

In truth, I could have filled page upon page of disturbing content drawn from anorexia related posts across social media platforms, which when actively searched for, do nothing but reinforce the mindset of someone captured by this condition. The majority of us, with absolutely no intention of running a similar search, are unlikely to have ever encountered this type of disturbing content. But for people suffering at the hands of this condition, they know it's there and exactly where to find it, with little to no safeguarding. The ease of access to this content only goes to reinforce a connection to the underlying addiction.

I ask… We're regulated to high heaven across all walks of daily life, so how the f*ck can these online platforms be allowed to let users, some desperately in need of help themselves, post this type of harmful content? In 2020, over 60% of those diagnosed with Anorexia Nervosa in the UK we're aged between 10 and 19. When I was in a really dark place, I was in my 30's. I'd been around the block a few times by then, so despite being highly vulnerable, I had a faint whisper of mature, rationale thinking in my head, warning me of the potential harm. With kids, they're incapable of seeing the danger through an adult's eyes. This makes my stomach churn when I think about of the potential harm being caused by allowing online 'addiction influencers' to be platformed.

2. The web not only provides a place of sanctuary for an addiction led illness, working to drag the unlucky 'host' deeper into its clasp…in cases, it actively hunts down victims of addiction. Shortly after finishing my research on gambling companies (supporting chapter 8), I was bombarded with online ads from pretty much all of the mainstream bookmakers, stalking me wherever I turned on my internet journey. Phone, tablet, or laptop, like most of us, all synced to the same Apple/Google ID, opened the door to a stream of free bets offers, extended odds, and a vast array of combinations on the next Premier League game.

If tobacco advertising can be banned in an effort to protect our physical health, why haven't other industries that are clearly linked harmful mental health conditions also been regulated in the same way? Like all these things, the answer will be simple… just follow the money!

The sheer level of sophistication built into internet algorithms scares the living daylights out of me. Ever had what you thought was a private conversation in the comfort of your own home about buying something with a smart speaker in ear shot, only to face a bombardment of enticing ads for that very item the next time you open the laptop? The point here, which I'm hoping is clear, is that when desperately trying to distance yourself from the draw of a crippling addiction, it's f*cking tragic that you can face being actively stalked, which does nothing more than reinforce the already connected self-harming behaviors.

You'll never see it as a written objective in the glossy strategic plans approved by the Boards of global tech giants, but it's clear they're all hooked on the opportunity presented by monetising the growing 'addiction' sector. Unless swift and very firm action is taken to regulate, I can only see the scale of the current problem getting worse.

Final Points

This has been by far and away the trickiest chapter for me to write, with a multitude of edits driven by a genuine fear that my honesty could be interpreted as carrying an intentionally offensive undertone. That said, the progressive deterioration we've witnessed in societal mental health over recent years is one hell of a tough subject to tackle without honesty!

I'd naturally expect some, possibly a large proportion of readers to disagree with some, possibly all of the views I've laid out in this chapter. This in itself is a positive thing, reinforcing my point about the importance that once again society should make space for debate instead of shutting the door on opinions even when supported by rationale. Where I'm personally wrong, I genuinely want to be educated. But my opinion can't change if I don't feel capable of openly expressing it!

There's a whole world of sh*t out there that a solitary individual is wholly incapable of controlling... wars, pandemics, parliamentary f*ck-wits, economic turmoil, social media etc. What is entirely within our own grasp of control is how we react to the uncontrollable. The challenge we face in 21st century is that life is running away from us at 100mph, making it impossible at times to stop and notice the things that adversely affect our thinking and behaviours. This in itself can make it incredibly hard to respond in a rational manner.

Despite the multitude of faults in our world today, just like the fallible nature of the humans that call this planet our home, a lot of good also remains out there... it's far too easy to always revert to the negatives! With a few tweaks here and there, some bigger than others, I genuinely believe that we can start to live with the greater degree of collectiveness (alongside our differences) ... but we all have to own the change!

CHAPTER 19
The Grievance

Pathological Narcissism

"... when narcissistic traits impair a person's daily functioning. That dysfunction typically causes friction in relationships due to the pathological narcissist's lack of empathy. It may also manifest as antagonism, fueled by grandiosity and attention-seeking. In seeing themselves as superior, the pathological narcissist naturally views everyone else as inferior and may be intolerant of disagreement or questioning."

PsychologyToday.com

OR

Moral Turpitude

"Conduct that is believed to be contrary to community standards of honesty, good morals, or justice."

LegalDictionary.net

Although I prefer:

*"You f*ck people, f*ck people over, and don't give a f*ck"*

Thomas Shelby Peaky Blinders
(Season 6, Episode 2)

Imagine a scenario where you find yourself in a position falsely accused of wrongful doing, the severity of the allegations resulting in a formal investigation into actions that would conflict with every part of your core value system!

Whilst writing this book I've been served up one hell of a f**cking treat wholly aligned with said scenario, which left me, totally innocent of all accusations, grappling in a battle to clear my name.

As if the last 6 months haven't been testing enough whilst simultaneously in a fight to challenge my now documented deep rooted personal issues covered in earlier chapters and hold down demanding professional and home lives, my toughest challenge turned out to be sat on a very different battle front... one that has without doubt tested my resolve to breaking point and at times ran the distinct risk of a relapse into the unhealthy ways of coping I've used in the past to cope with stress and anxiety.

I've intentionally held back from making any reference to this specific situation until now, the core subject of the book giving me with a very welcome distraction from the wider sh*t I've been dealing with. Added to this I couldn't embark on the subject matter, which does in fact carry distinct parallels with broader theme of this book, until my innocence had been proved. I've remained patient, knowing it was only a matter of time!

The said situation concerns a recent set of events in my professional life, so requires a careful approach in terms of my choice of words used in what is a very public domain. By deciding to publicise the experience, even with extreme caution, I'm know that taking a big gamble, presenting a potential risk to my future job security. That said, the distinct parallels I can draw between recent events and the broader theme of this book has left my desire for openness outweighing the potentially more rational decision to avoid risk. The harsh reality is that my own experience could easily happen to anyone and if the starting point of the 'accused' is deemed 'stable yet mentally fragile', this type of situation could end up being the tipping point... possibly down a path towards 'health destroying' coping mechanisms!

A year ago, I moved into a new role at work which came with some new people reporting into me. Motivation in a professional sense varies from one person to another, the usual suspects being the opportunity to develop new technical skills or simply to climb the career ladder, earning more money on the way up. Both carry weight (excuse the pun) in my list of drivers, but neither top the list. Top of my list by a long distance is the opportunity that work provides to forge and grow strong relationships. I like understanding other people and experience tells me that solid relationships are hell of an influential tool when it comes to simply getting sh*t done… especially in my line of work. Being just as fallible as any other person, I'm grounded enough to recognise that I'm way off being the perfect leadership role-model, but on balance, like to think of myself as an accountant who carries above average levels of empathy and compassion… versus the stereotype that accompanies my professional!

On starting the new job one of my new direct reports turned out to be someone I'd crossed paths with on a prior work project, and if I'm being entirely honest, I was left far from impressed by what I saw as a distinct lack of effort on their part. That said, I've never been one to let a first impression cement into hardened view, so started the new working relationship with a blank canvas for my mind to paint over time.

Four months into the new role with my feet finally starting to settle under the table, despite best efforts, the individual's overall contribution did nothing but reinforce that first impression, pointing to an issue of underperformance. At the same time, the rest of my team were working their ar*es off, showing themselves to be a genuine credit to the business.

Having decided to do a little digging around to establish whether the issue was a new one or had been there for some time it emerged that 'performance' discussions had taken place with the individual, but nothing formal had ever been done to address the problem. For whatever reason, which I initially thought was down to lack of time, the failure to address the challenge at the point it first presented ended up making it a lot harder to rectify ... although the events that would ultimately unfold probably explain why there could have been a lack of willingness to address through the appropriate policy channels in the past!

As someone who genuinely gives a sh*t about people I hope my team see me as a supportive manager who's willing to lead from the front and doesn't mind getting his hands covered in cr*p if it supports the team cause. This is a conscious go-to approach I take in the belief that builds a motivated environment where everyone pulls their weight... something that's personally important in the broader sense of life. If there's a weak link in a team, with no sign that it's down to a gap in capability (which support can close) and all signs pointing to a simple case of poor motivation and behaviours, it has to be addressed! Sitting back and ignoring the problem helps no one, running the distinct risk that other team members become hacked off by weak management that leaves them having to overcompensate just to fill the void. In this type of situation, it's only a matter of time before the good 'troops' vote with their feet with resignation letters. Pretty simple stuff that applies to any team setting, but in my humble opinion this type of issue is more common than recognised in the workplace.

I'm not someone to shy away from a challenge, so having spoken to HR and been advised to follow the process set out in the 'Performance Policy', I kicked off the early stages of the process with said individual with a **genuine** intent to support them in lifting their performance to align business needs. No respectable leader with an ounce of humility would relish the prospect of entering this type of process, knowing if things don't proceed down the intended path, it can result in a long and drawn-out ordeal that benefits neither party in the process. It's time consuming, compounds the pressure felt in an already hectic work setting, and to be frank, it's hardly a pleasant thing to tell that someone that their performance isn't hitting the mark… but sometimes, it's a necessary evil!

A month into the process and with best endeavours clear from my side (laying out plans, agreeing targets, offering support, and trying to keep discussions positive) it became abundantly clear that all advice was being ignored with no intent shown from the other side to bridge the gap. It was blindingly obvious that I wasn't dealing with capability issue. I was dealing with nothing more than poor behaviours, leaving me with one of two choices… ignore the issue (the easy option) or formalise the process by moving to the next stage in the company policy (the tough option!).

Taking this kind of process down a more formal route is not only a last resort (for any right-minded leader), but also a huge drain on time, especially when it comes to the now common 'process mill' used by modern day corporate business. Big companies are sh*t scared of any risk that action (even if rightful) leads to an employment tribunal. This has left many HR departments fuelled by what I can only describe as an acute case of anxiety (I know the feeling) that's produced excessive levels of treacle like red tape for a manager to wade through… whilst the demands from the day job stay the same!

The all too often lack of support a manager gets, partly down to a cross industry move towards slimmed down 'self-service' HR models (i.e. if you need something done, do it the f*ck yourself!), goes some way to explain why leaders often shy away from addressing performance issues. They simply haven't got the mental capacity or bandwidth to manage the process set out by company policy. Alongside this, few (including myself) are armed with a detailed understanding of UK employment law, leaving them fully exposed to being tripped up by simply applying common sense. It's no wonder that UK productivity statistics are as shocking as they are when leaders are expected match the likes of Colin Jackson when it comes to clearing the hurdles in their way when addressing performance issues.

I knew the specific case I was dealing with would place a big strain on my time and energy, but I had no idea the strain would ultimately trample all over my state of mind. With no foresight of what would ensue, I ploughed ahead, sticking my spam (forehead) above the parapet by completing the necessary paperwork recommending a move to a formal stage of review. This was the point that things quickly turned nasty!

Within no time after sitting down with said individual to inform them that I was moving to a formal stage of review, I get a call from my boss notifying me that they had raised a formal grievance against me, citing accusations of racism and agism on my part. For obvious reasons I can't give away any specific details, but I'm safe by saying that it was more or less impossible for either of the accusation boxes to actually be ticked with any credibility.

On receiving the news my initial reaction wasn't one of surprise. I suspected the person in question would try to turn the 'system' on its head in an attempt to weaponise it against me! At the same time, I honestly thought the 'system' would also be there to support me. Admittedly, at that point my expectations on the level of support I'd receive were probably a little too ambitious, hoping that HR would see right through the (false) accusations by immediately throwing the grievance out of the window, citing a lack of evidence to support the accusations pointed in my direction. Afterall, I knew there wasn't any evidence… because **I hadn't actually done anything wrong**. Once I'd managed to put my rational head back on I completely understood why HR informed me that I was facing an internal investigation, which I genuinely thought would be done and dusted in no time. I mean, it's not a good look if you've got a genuine racist on the payroll and you fail to address the problem quickly! But boy, how wrong was I when it came to the anticipated timeline.

The next 3 and a half months proved to be f*cking hellish at times! It took weeks for recorded interviews to be conducted, evidence to be assessed (which didn't actually exist) and finally to conclude that the allegations would not be upheld (i.e., I was innocent of any wrongdoing). While the system dragged its stiletto like heals, I was left in no man's land retaining line management oversight of someone who'd not only made false allegations that threatened to ruin a reputation that I'd worked f*cking hard over to build over many years, but also did their upmost to make my working life as difficult as possible! Outside of a working environment, you'd be forgiven for giving a straight two barrels worth to anyone who'd treated you in a similar fashion. However much I wanted to react as my instinct demanded, doing so in a professional setting would have left me facing a charge of gross misconduct, something I strongly suspect is exactly what said individual wanted!

Thinking I was now **rightfully** in the clear to proceed with the process I'd legitimately started, I get an email informing me that the grievance outcome had been appealed by the accuser. At this point, I rightfully/wrongfully thought that HR would tell them to (politely) f*ck-off. Unfortunately, this wasn't to be, with the 'squeaky bums' in 'Robot Resources' confirming the appeal would duly be reviewed… despite the lack of any original nor new evidence to substantiate the accusations pointed in my direction.

Qu another 2 months waiting for justice, my sanity intentionally being tested on a daily basis by said individual who was clearly making every effort to corner me into making a mistake that would evidence some kind of wrongdoing. Alongside the normal pressures from work and home life, the added stress from the overall injustice of the situation sparked life into the hardcore addiction led thoughts I'd experienced in yesteryear, **demanding** that I exercise at every opportunity whilst slashing my calorie intake… in bid to regain control. Thankfully, despite a couple of hiccups, I managed to stop the thinking from translating into action.

I voiced my concern with HR that after everything that had happened, I was left to work in close proximity to someone who had not only accused me of being a racist but was also doing their upmost to make my working life as difficult as possible using an armory of disruptive passive aggressive tactics. What option did the 'system' offer up? "You're well within your right to raise a counter-grievance"!

I mean, for f*ck sake! At this point, with the distraction from the experience starving other members of the team of my time and support + my own output starting to suffer I thought I'd get some support, not pursue childish playground tactics with a 'I said, they said' strategy. And then there's the unspoken risk of reputational damage on my part if I were seen to elongate the process with a 'tit for tat' counter-grievance.

If you're of a certain pay grade is there an unwritten rule that means you're somehow immune to normal levels of human vulnerability?

Finally, just before Christmas, I get an email from HR… After months investigating the matter, the original decision had **yet again** been upheld (i.e., I remained innocent). If it hadn't been for the persistence of my boss who stepped in to push for the matter to be concluded one way or another, I'm convinced the process would have dragged on even longer.

I knew all along that the decision reached would arrive at some point, envisaging it would spark a well-earned celebration. But when it arrived, it proved to be one f*cking big anti-climax, mainly because despite preceding events, there was an expectation that things would return to "normal". Yep, you got it, said person would continuing to report into me just like nothing had ever happened.

Maybe it's down to my working class roots that makes trust of paramount importance to me, but I'd say the decision would have justified a point-blank refusal to continue working with the individual. But what good would this have done? I'd have left another member of the wider leadership team exposed to the real risk of another grievance if they'd tried to address the original problem. Alongside this, I strongly suspect that I'd have been seen as an antagonist, even if for wholly justifiable reasons. One thing's for sure, creating the perception that you're a disrupter, even if with the right intent, won't do your future prospects any favours in a large corporate business. When everyone is under the cosh, trying to keep on top of workloads, causing a 'scene' is an all-round pretty sh*t look!

I wouldn't blame you for thinking "this guy has one hell of a bitter taste in his mouth displaying narcissistic traits with the "me, me, me" script". Having re-read the preceding paragraphs, I'd acknowledge this as a wholly justifiable point of view. But if this is the conclusion you've come to, the overarching point has been missed (or I've been failed to get it across!).

Despite the cognitive shortcomings in my past, most (but not all) of which are thankfully behind me, I'm actually a pretty tough nut to crack. But what if I wasn't able to cope? What if the events I've had to deal with this year had happened when I was in a more vulnerable disposition? This begs the question... how do others out there facing similar circumstances in the workplace cope with the inevitable strain on their mental health?

Employers rightfully expect leaders like me to deal with

underperforming employees. But they also expect leaders, often in their position due to the expertise held in a field of discipline and not for their ability to act in the capacity of a psychologist, to simply deal with extreme cases involving false accusations of wrongdoing. All too often, a leader has neither the sufficient training and support to deal with this type of situation, nor do they have the bandwidth to manage it alongside a hectic day job. The harsh reality is the 'accused' is more or less left to crack on with it, leaving them exposed to 'cracking' during the process.

I can assure you that this hasn't just been a rant targeted at the arguably unintended shortcomings on the part of my employer. For my sake, I sincerely hope they don't see it that way! Like most other corporate businesses, the internal HR infrastructure and supporting policies are set-up with one aim in mind… to mitigate the risk of an employment tribunal and any associated reputational damage this could cause. I'm an accountant, so I'm pretty well versed to protecting assets and mitigating business risk… I get why it works the way it does, but at the same time, it doesn't make it right!

Whilst it probably sounds sadistic (although unintentionally), the good thing (which is actually bad) is that I appear to be far from alone. I've spoken to, and heard second hand, about other leaders who've also faced allegations wrongdoing, some far worse than those pointed at me. The common themes that stand out in each case are (1) all were found to be innocent, and (2) in cases, the accuser left the company with a 'golden handshake' (a pay-off) … the later making a mockery of the whole situation!

Whilst the likelihood is this type of situation probably remains low in numbers when looking at UK employment in its entirety, I'd say it's likely to be a bigger problem than recognised. Why? Because in most instances, it's simply swept under the carpet!

My strong suspicion is the problem of false allegations of discrimination in the workplace, is on the rise… but it's a hypothesis that's virtually impossible to prove. I've searched high and low across the web and even trawled through the vast catalogue of ONS data, all to no avail.

You try a google search (I've tried countless variations of the same question), and it'll return pages of links to random HR articles giving insight on managing a grievance process, details of legislation in place to protect people from discrimination, and countless legal firms, who've clearly spotted a commercial opportunity to make a buck from both sides of any accusation. The simple fact is, there are no hard statistics, but there's a minefield of soundbites and pockets of government data that when combined to draw conclusions, would rightly be downplayed as circumstantial at best. In a modern world where wealth is now founded on data, why should it be so hard to address such a simple question? Because, from everything I can see there is no form of legal recourse for those falsely accused of discrimination, bullying or harassment in the workplace. No right to recourse = no data!

The only data I've managed to source, that could in some way support my suspicion that false accusations of discrimination are on the rise, is the number of newly registered UK employment tribunal cases, sourced from Ministry of Justice reports. This points to a 96% increase in new tribunal cases registered between 2014 and 2019, representing a 14.6% compound annual growth rate (the average rate of year-on-year growth).

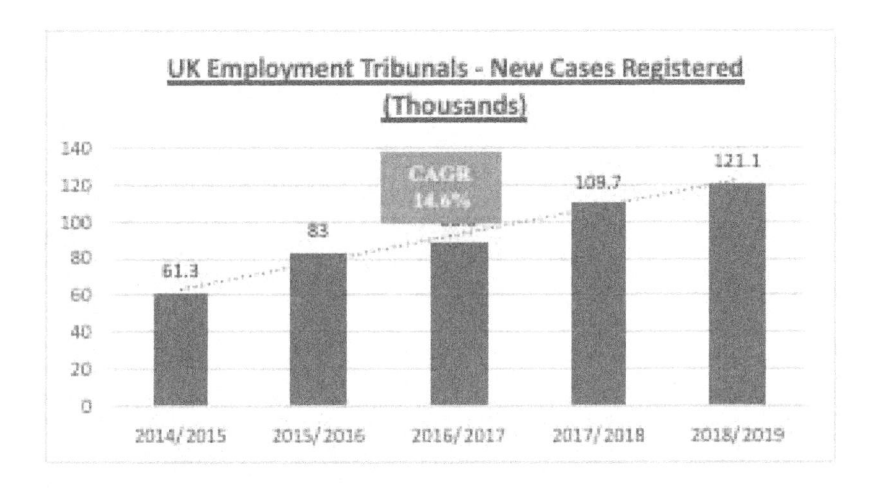

UK Employment Tribunals - New Cases Registered (Thousands)

2014/2015	2015/2016	2016/2017	2017/2018	2018/2019
61.3	83		109.7	121.1

CAGR 14.6%

* Source: gov.uk

** Data is available for 2020/2021 but purposefully omitted owing to the likely distortion caused by changes to work related conditions during the pandemic.

Using this data as hard evidence to justify my hypothesis is as crumbly as a Cadburys flake (I know, a cr*p analogy, but I couldn't think of anything better). Afterall, it includes all types of employment disputes (i.e., not just those centered on discrimination) and based on those cases with a foundation to support a claim going to tribunal (i.e., it excludes most/all cases where an internal grievance process has deemed that no offence has occurred, or where the charge has been upheld and the business has dealt with it appropriately). But at a macro level, it could point (albeit loosely) to a trend. This sentiment is supported by an article published by HR Magazine (September 2021) quoting that with the use of data sourced from a Freedom of Information request, it was found that "Employment tribunals in the UK saw a 48% rise in the number of race discrimination claims in 2020". The theme is further supported by a discussion I recently had with an unnamed 'in the know expert' at work, revealing that at any time there are circa 400 live grievances cases being managed, the majority of which are linked to accusations of discrimination.

So, is the UK workplace becoming an increasingly discriminatory environment to earn a living? I can only answer this question based on the developments I've witnessed over recent years, which points to the UK working environment being more inclusive than ever. With this in mind, the statistics simply don't make sense!

Yet again, I'm feeling an overwhelming urge to validate my very genuine support for of our nation's strive towards creating a more diverse and inclusive (D&I) society. But I know that any opinion that steps into this subject matter, even if approached with the best intent, can easily be taken out of context.

I've personally benefited from the greater focus on D&I, the reduced stigma associated with mental illness making it safer for me to publicly 'come out' as a male anorectic. We must continue working towards a more equitable landscape across all walks of life, not for you or I, but to build an even platform for our children and grandchildren. At the same time, I don't feel that equality can be achieved if the roadmap to societal balance can in parts discriminate against the majority. The path to a genuine **meritocracy** is the answer, something which cannot be achieved overnight using tools like 'positive discrimination' which I've always viewed as a conflicting term… how can any form of discrimination be positive?

My observation, which could appear a little catastrophic, but remains genuine, is that the white British male is increasingly being painted as the architype misogynist and racist bigot. Yes, there are men out there who are complete f*cking ar*holes with a minority falling into the 'pure evil category'… but surely, they must remain in the minority? A topical case in point would be the widely publicised culture issues in the Metropolitan Police force. Guys like Wayne Cousins and David Carrick deserve to get everything that prison dishes up for them to make them pay for their crimes (I'll let you use your imagination). But these sickening high-profile cases don't mean all policeman in the Met should be feared by women... which is the picture that's been painted across media platforms.

Whether you agree with me or not, I can tell you that anxiety in the everyday, respectable British guy is definitely on the rise, often through fear of well-intended words or actions causing offence, running the risk of it leading to life changing consequences. When the definition of offence isn't binary, meaning one person's joke is another person's insult, it's bl**dy tough for the 'good guy' to navigate his way through life without an innocent but potentially fatal slip. I've personally got to the stage now where feel uneasy saying a simple "good evening" when passing a woman on an evening dog walk. I now cross the road, making every effort to illustrate that I pose absolutely no threat to their safety.

This anxiety is spilling into the professional environment, evidenced by a poll carried out in the US by Forbes Magazine, revealing that 82% of men are worried about women making false allegations of harassment or assault at work. On the assumption that the percentage of American guys fitting the profile of a misogynist is significantly less than 82% (I'd hope), where does this leave the respectable men among those polled? ... some anxious, but all distracted to a varying extent, from fully focusing on the demands of their job.

'Micro-aggressions' have emerged as a key area of focus in the workplace, aiming to mitigate the risk of causing offense and from there reduce the risk of an employment tribunal down the line. Look at someone with an uninviting facial expression, or mis-pronounce someone's name (as I do regularly) or pronoun, and you could face accusations of bullying.

Is it me or has any common sense that society once had gradually evaporated over recent years? If I were to (not that I would) stare down someone in the office like I was about to punch them square between the eyes, I'd expect to be pulled up. But what if I'm just having a bad day, as we all experience from time to time, and I'm walking through the office immersed in whatever internal sh*t I'm dealing with, looking thoroughly hacked off? Would a frown or lack of eye contact make me a bully? Maybe the answer is that employers should install 'happy pill' dispensers for parents to immediately lift them from the stress we all feel after a cr*p school run first thing in the day?

For me, it's saddening inditement of where things have got to, that even if it does relate to a small percentage of cases, legislation and internal policy aimed at protecting genuinely vulnerable people, is in cases being weaponised against innocent people in the workplace. If you want further evidence of the real problem this presents, look no further than the growth in businesses and charities set up to support those protesting their innocence against the type of false accusations I encountered this year (e.g., freespeechunion.org).

It is my belief that until we start to see a more commonsense approach to managing the change, I wholeheartedly believe is **needed** to drive greater equality for all in society, we are likely to see the weaponisation of well-intended legislation and internal company policy grow… by the kind of ^&%$£er who raised the grievance against me. Until common sense prevails, the likelihood is that we'll continue to see a deterioration in the mental health of those ill-equipped to deal with the emotional impact this type of situation causes.

Absolute f*cking Madness!

BACK TO WHERE I BEGAN

CHAPTER 20
78kg

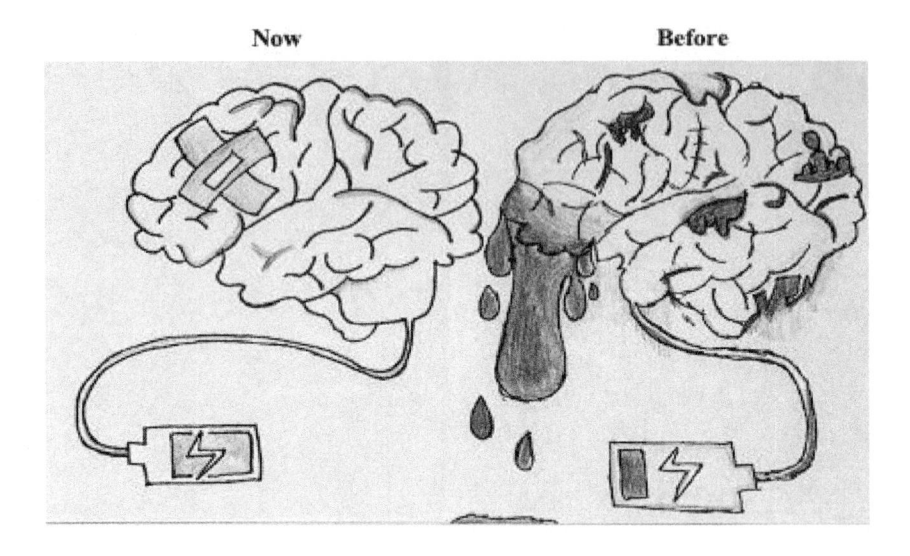

Now　　　　　　　　　　　Before

Illustrated by: *My Daughter*

Back in 2015, just before anorexia nervosa took a hold of my life, I was a fit and healthy 36-year-old man, weighing in at 78kg (12 stone 5 pounds in 'old money'). After what's now been an eight-year slog, two spent in complete denial that I ever had a problem, four spent in a stable yet barely functioning state, and a final two pushing towards recovery, I finally find myself back to where I began (78kg).

A heightened level of frustration was probably the main thing that led me to start writing this book, hacked off at myself for wasting too long living in a state of stagnation. My weight remained fixed at 73kg, the engine running on the dregs of the tank, leaving my body and state of mind ill-equipped to manage day-to-day life with the strength and composure required.

You've gone to the effort to read this book, so I'd sympathise if you may be thinking it's been a f*cking waste of time, with all those words add up to a measly 5kg of weight gain! In a desperate bid to temper any feelings of disappointment, the journey from a mere 63kg back in 2015 to a 73kg in 2022 was a f*cking tough slog… but the final 5kg has felt a lot harder! Most importantly, the gain has finally tipped me back into the safety zone!

So, what difference has a mere 5kg of weight gain made to my life?

I've thought long and hard about how to answer this question, not because the difference it's made hasn't been nothing but positive. My deeper thinking than probably necessary (that's me!) is solely down to the single objective I set myself when I started to write this book…. that I would paint a picture of reality rather than depict the set of evangelical outcomes I've observed in other 'self-help' books. I'm a self-confessed sceptic and all round realist! I recognise that quick fixes don't exist in game of life we're all playing, so I'd be breaking every rule in my moral 'rule book' if I were to depict a utopian life should you decide to follow suit in applying the principles of marginal gains theory in a bid to remove addiction from your life.

Getting back to the point by (finally) addressing the question at hand… the stand-out difference to my life by finally reaching a healthy weight is my newfound level of resilience. I feel more energised, giving me the focus to deal with the day to day demands of a hectic life. This has arrived with a level of cognitive strength that's allowed me to deal with professional and personal challenges with essential rational thinking (although my boss may argue otherwise).

The road back to health hasn't transformed this sceptic into a happy-clappy 'tree hugging' activist but it's given me a sense of contentment with life that I've honestly not felt for years. To help illustrate, I'd look no further than the growing ease I feel in 'housing' a larger (and healthier) body mass. This alone represents a huge leap forward from all those years spent petrified of a single decimal increase registered by those f*cking electric scales.

Using a more tangible example to help illustrate, I'd look no further than a recent family holiday, our first abroad since 2019. We could never be ar*ed with overseas travel during the pandemic, given the ever-changing list of red and green destinations running the risk of ending up stranded, vaccine passport red tape, and the principle I couldn't bring myself to line the pockets of the Covid-19 testing racket. Most important of all, we weren't prepared to risk being forced into UK quarantine having to pay £200 a night to stay in a grotty airport hotel that charged £50 pre-pandemic. F*ck that!

Our first venture from UK shores saw us travel to Antalya (Turkey) at Easter, staying in one of the vast number of all-inclusive resorts that line the sandy beaches. It's a gut-wrenching admission to make but family holidays between 2014-2019 were far from the enjoyable experience they should have been. The impact from my illness on the family, particularly my loving wife, has left me with nothing but feelings of guilt from to all those holidays overshadowed by an edgy atmosphere. Back then I hated every second of what should have been a hard-earned time of enjoyment for all the family, but it was hell for me living in an environment with an abundance of food and hotel guests (deservedly) 'filling their boots' in the buffet restaurant and 24/7 snack bars. The tension this created was felt by all, especially my wife, who I know felt forced simultaneously tiptoe around me whilst putting on a brave face for the kids (not that she ever complained).

This year's holiday was different! For the first time in years **I genuinely** enjoyed myself, managing to eat well (versus pinning myself to the salad bar), and despite the odd spat between a teenage daughter and approaching teenage son, we had a brilliant time… exactly the way it should be! I even relaxed a little, a pre-requisite on the itinerary of a resort-based holiday, sticking two fingers up to the 'must' to partake in strenuous levels of exercise… a box I'd have historically ticked every day, usually in blistering midday heat. I managed to limit myself to a 20min daily swim in what turned out to be a f*cking freezing pool… fooled by my wife who was adamant that all outdoor Turkish swimming pools are heated!

I've felt a big step change in my life since I started writing this book. But the notable elephant that remains in the room is whether anorexia nervosa has actually packed its bags and left my life for good? Before addressing the elephant, I should touch on my original perceived outcome if I were to reach the not so dizzy heights of my pre eating disorder weight (which I have). I'd envisaged what I can only describe as one of those perfect fairy tale endings where, as if by magic, my addiction would miraculously dissipate and leave me forever. The reality is that whilst I'm now lightyears ahead of where I stood not so long ago, Walt Disney endings bear little resemblance to the reality of life.

I have repaired my physical and mental health to the extent that I've finally passed an MOT with some fuel in the tank. At the same time, I've had to come to terms with the fact that whilst my illness no longer dominates my life, the presence anorexia nervosa is unlikely to ever be fully erased.

The general perception is that 'recovery' from an eating disorder like anorexia is in some way different to recovering from an addiction to drugs or alcohol. The fact is, **it's exactly the same!** Once an addict, always an addict, whether you're sat firmly on the wagon, or fallen flat on your face! This doesn't mean the determination in the fight to break free should ever be lost! In my case I take comfort from the fact I'm now firmly on the wagon, feet up in business class feeling a sense of strength and focus that should prevent me from ever falling off it.

Yes, I am still exercising more that your 'average Joe', the difference between my past and the present being that this part of my life is now firmly under control, using it stimulate rather than destroy me. Last week I ran in my first race since I set my personal best marathon time back in 2014 (8 years ago). I joined a team of colleagues from work at the annual JP Morgan London Battersea Park run. I'm not sure why the hell I agreed to take part, knowing that based on where I was a mere two years ago, it could be like a recovering alcoholic saying yes to a single glass of wine. That said, whilst the event proved to be great in terms of the laugh had with my teammates, I hated every minute of the run… mainly because at 29mins 30sec, I was over 10 minutes slower than I used to be. I can honestly say that if I were that recovering alcoholic, the wine that evening was like sipping from a glass of malt vinegar!

By far and away the biggest change I've made in my bid to replenish the 'heath' I lost to addiction has been the gradual yet consistent increase in my daily nourishment… to the point where it finally exceeded the calories burnt through a controlled level of exercise, making a decent amount of weight gain possible. Don't get me wrong, the long-standing carte blanche ban remains on the consumption most of the processed sh*t our fast food nation is now hooked on (i.e. you won't see me anywhere near a McDonalds) … but I'm perfectly okay with, knowing that what I've actually done has worked.

I look at myself now, 45 years old, carrying a far higher density of grey on top and a few extra frowning induced wrinkles than I had back in 2015/16 … but I feel a lot healthier within. Putting aside the arduous journey to finally reach a minimum acceptable weight, my unfortunate but overwhelming point of reflection is the precious time I lost to a deep-rooted addiction… time I'll never get back. Feelings of regret, self-loathing, even anger, are perfectly understandable, being the usual 'go to' places for human thinking when reflecting in such a way. But I hold solace by recognising that I was mentally ill for an extended period, and I'm determined to use the years I lost to addiction as the fuel I need to stop me from ever going back there again. I cannot and will not lose any more precious years, wanting to see my kids grow up and make their own way in the world, and with any luck my wife and I grow old gracefully... assuming she's also up for it ☺!

I often think about the sense of irony that accompanies a journey back from the depths of anorexia nervosa. The path goes against every part of the daily script we're bombarded with, and the mantra applied to most forms of addiction recovery... both push for abstinence! Public Health authorities constantly push the hard message that our ever more obese nation should abstain from junk and sugar, and recovery from the likes of alcohol and gambling addiction is predicated on giving up. Recovering from anorexia nervosa is predicated on the complete opposite, doing more (increasing calorific intake) rather than less. Merely an observation which helps to cast light on the uphill challenge faced on the journey from an anorexia to a freer life.

Before stepping into the usual final parting words and acknowledgements, I'll touch on some good news I received only yesterday. Over the last four month's (yes four!), I've been going through what I can only describe as the most thorough interview process for a new job. After no less than 5 interviews, including a 2.5-hour grilling from a business psychologist (akin to what we see at the penultimate stage of 'The Apprentice'), I've been offered and accepted the position of CFO (Chief Financial Officer) working for a different division of the business I've been at since 2019. During the interview process, I actually made a point of being very open about my once wedded relationship with anorexia nervosa, which some of my trusted advisors deemed a risky tactic. For me, it was simply a test to establish whether those interviewing me could actually see through the mental health alarm bells and make a judgement based on my personality and ability rather than my history with an eating disorder. All I can say is fair play to the company…. I'm now looking forward to joining them!

PARTING WORDS

CHAPTER 21
Reflections & Advice

After nearly two and a half years in the making I'm nearing the end of my first adventure with words!

Simultaneously juggling the demands of a pretty intense job whilst doing my best to be a half decent partner and parent is an everyday test for most. Finding additional space to focus on journaling has without doubt required a whole new level of determination! Still, it's kept me quiet, something my wife appreciates (☺), and given my kids plenty of ammunition to take the p*ss out their old man... "What the hell have you got to write about would be of interest to anyone else? You're just a lanky accountant!". If only they knew! One day, hopefully when they're a little older, I hope they have a go at reading it themselves, knowing its likely to open their eyes to some things they never knew about their 'bean counter' dad.

A few months ago, at the ripe old age of 45, I received a long-suspected dyslexia diagnosis which makes completing this book feel like a solid self-accomplishment. Whether the book actually makes f*cking any sense is an entirely different matter! ☺

The results from the dyslexia test also pointed towards a potential ADHD diagnosis. Having battled to secure an ADHD test through the NHS, this was subsequently confirmed. If you're wondering what purpose there is in mentioning this, don't worry, I've no intention at this stage of wearing my diagnosis like a badge of honour in a bid to earn what have become valuable neurodiversity points across social media platforms☺. For me, it helps to add some much needed additional context that could explain why I've encountered challenges in my past. It also sheds light on why I struggled to form the essential rational thinking that could well have put a stop to some of the challenges I've encountered before they escalated into crisis situations. One thing's for sure, it's sparked a whole new level of interest into the correlation between neurodiversity and addiction:

> *"Neurodivergent individuals, such as those with autism spectrum disorder or ADHD, are more susceptible to developing eating disorders due to their unique cognitive and sensory processing differences. Therefore, it is crucial for mental health professionals to receive specialised training in working with this population... neurodivergent individuals often exhibit atypical behaviours and communication styles that can be misinterpreted by professionals unfamiliar with their neurology. For instance, repetitive behaviours... may be mistaken for obsessive-compulsive disorder symptoms related to eating disorders... neurodivergent individuals may have sensory sensitivities that impact their relationship with food."*
>
> *Bernie Wright Counsellor/Clinical Supervisor/Specialist in Eating Disorders & Distressed Eating*
> *(My Practitioner between 2016 and 2018)*

Any science linking neurodiversity and the propensity to be led down a path of addiction is 100% a subject I want to understand more about. Possibly the theme for a future book? For now, I'm taking a break from writing to focus on more important things in life; family and the dog! The saving grace for now is that my newfound neurodivergent status (ADHD & Dyslexia) means I hold the f*cking trump card should anyone attempt to find fault in this book's 'SPAG' (spelling, punctuation, and gramma)! ☺

I set out to try and make the content in this book as broad as possible, covering a lot of content to take in and digest. Yes, I've aired some arguably controversial opinions in a time where diverse opinions aren't always welcome, but I'm cool with the fact that disagreement is just part of life. If you've got this far, opinions clearly haven't stopped you from ploughing on to the end of what's been very real account of a situation in life that continues to affect an increasing number of people.

If you're living with similar challenges to those I've drawn upon from my own experience, I'm hoping that a few final pointers and words of reflection will help nudge you into the first or next stage of your own personal recovery journey:

1. Applying marginal gains theory <u>does</u> work: If you strive for overnight perfection from the outset, the chances are that you'll fail at the first hurdle. If your life is controlled by addiction led behaviors, you need to accept that your thinking is more than likely to be hardwired. Contrary to the lightning speed we now expect to address other modern-day problems, there's no quick fix available for this one! Patience is critical if when taking those small, yet consistent steps forward to untangle the wiring, helping to put your life back on track.

2. Humankind waits for a crisis before it responds: For Christ's sake, if you've read this book as someone who's generally okay in life but you carry an addictive personality (we all know who we are!), keep a close eye on yourself! Noticing and reigning in the "musts" before they reach crisis point is a lot f*cking easier than having to haul yourself out of a deep crisis down the line. I'd strongly urge you to use my story as a stark warning of what can happen when things get out of control. If you've read this as an observer having seen an increasing connection between a friend/loved one and unhealthy behaviors, make sure you pluck up the courage to check in with them. As someone who is close to them, you'll know the difference between denial and a genuine "yeah, I'm okay".

3. Don't rely on others to fix your problems: This is a f*cking tough message to hear when you're personally in a bad place, but the fact is, only you can own the changes required to address your problems. Broadly speaking, I'd say that society has moved to a place in the last couple of decades where we shift accountability to others (family/the state/our employer) for sorting out our personal sh*t… it's always someone else's problem to address. A few years back I fell into the same camp, wasting years expecting the NHS to come to the rescue with a magical cure that would fix me. Yes, we should absolutely reach out when help is needed, but we should also acknowledge that the NHS is now f*cked! With demand for mental health support outstripping supply in multiples, you should absolutely demand medical help, but at the same time I'd urge you to do everything you can to muster some strength to start working with yourself. It might only help stablise a gradual decline, but that's more than good enough while you wait for help to arrive.

So here we are, approaching the end of my first venture into the world of literacy. Based on my prior reading, I'd say it's delivered a very different product to other books in the self-help genre… down to earth, written by someone who hasn't promised you a quick fix, but I can promise that if you're willing to put in the hard yards, you can fix things!

Goodluck, stay strong, and remember… **never, ever f*cking give-up!**

ACKNOWLEDGEMENTS

&

REMEMBERING THE DEPARTED

CHAPTER 22
Gratitude
(Where Thoroughly Deserved)

In keeping with the tradition of biographical literature, the time has arrived to recognise a small number of very important people for their contribution and support over the years in my (now) publicised battle with an eating disorder. Without their help, with two of them supporting in a rather odd way, my personal circumstances could well have looked very different to how they stand today.

<u>Family</u>

My wife, whom I'll finally name as Kerry, has undoubtably played the biggest and most influential role, helping to guide me on every step of what's been an arduous journey towards contentment. Despite every attempt that anorexia nervosa made to obliterate our marriage, she stuck by me through thick and thin whilst somehow finding additional strength to be the best mum ever to our kids during times when I was nothing but a wholly absent parent. I know just how she suffered during those dark days and yearn one day to unpack her personal experience as an innocent bystander living with an addict. At the same time, I respect her general stance that this particular part of our past isn't a subject matter she likes to talk about. She's, someone I admire and love immensely, carrying a desire to focus on 'what next' rather than 'what happened'.

Next in line are my mum and stepdad. Again, they've been through a lot, my mum left nearly broken by what saw become of her son, my stepdad left to pick up the pieces in his own unique and caring way. I hate to think about the pain and worry my illness created for two people who should have been relaxing in later life. But however hard it got they were always there for me when needed. At my lowest, when things were exceptionally hard at home for Kerry and the kids, they gave me a place to stay, helping to remove the toxicity of addiction from the family home. My mum, who'll be 70 next year, looks visibly more relaxed when I see her now… a stark contrast from the distraught expression I'd get when she embraced a skeleton on arrival to visit them in the past.

Next, I must thank my daughter for her artistic contribution towards this book. I challenged myself long and hard about asking her to put pencil to paper on a handful of drawings, some arguably on the darker side of art. That said, she's always been artistic, unlike her father. Did she do it for the love of her dad? I'd like to think so but strongly suspect the cut in potential book royalties she negotiated was the primary reason for her decision to participate… a mindset I'm expecting will take her go far in life! ☺.

And finally, I thank my son for giving me the chance to see and be part of a solid father/son bond, the type I wish I'd had with my old man. He's a cheeky little g*t, publicly referring to his dad as "Mr Lanky" or "Peter Crouch" in front of his school friends and football teammates. But within that (approaching) teenage humour and sometimes lack of respect, we're building a relationship I hope will stand the test of time as best of mates.

Friends

Deep down, I'm a pretty solitary character. I've got loads of acquaintances but only a small handful of people I'd put into the bucket of people I enjoy spending time with, **and** I can rely upon when it comes to a favour. In-fact there's only two people I'd class as genuine mates, the kind you will be there for you in desperate times. One of them, Richard, who I first met at work back in 2007 is one of a rare breed of people we seldom encounter in life. He's someone with a genuine heart of gold, who has an all-round caring approach to life with absolutely no personal agenda or strings attached.

His masculine side probably won't like the fact that I'm depicting him in very public way as some kind of wet lettuce, so I'll set his masculine record straight by also acknowledging his Mr Miyagi speed when it comes to some good old fashioned man banter.

Owing to our busy work and family lives 'Rich' and I only meet up 4-5 times a year, each time parting with a post 4 pint promise to not leave it so long next time. In typical bloke fashion, we never do. The failed mutual commitment never matters as he's always been there for me whenever needed, in both darker and improving times. Knowing how busy he is I'd consciously avoid being overly needy during the bad times. The fact that I knew he'd have been if asked was a massive comfort in itself. He's a brilliant guy, who'd I'd honestly do anything for. Probably best that I leave the man love there to avoid the risk of making stomachs churn!

The Voices of Sanity

Now to the oddity… 'The Thought Police' podcast!

This became my weekly voice of sanity which has stayed with me since 2020. Presented by Mike Graham and Kevin O'Sullivan, two well-known presenters on Talk Radio/TV, this podcast has the solitary aim to smash through the increasingly restrictive woke boundary markers that now separate 'allowable' from 'genuine' free speech. Definitely not for the faint hearted and one to avoid for anyone easily offended by words. The gradual erosion of satire comedy over the last couple of decades may explain why those who may find it offensive are somewhat missing the point.

I don't believe for a second that some of the sentiment in 'Mike and Kev's' weekly cut-throat debate on topical news stories is pitched as they would in everyday life. The sentiment in the content is there with one aim in mind... to test the boundaries others are afraid to test. These guys wouldn't have the profile they've got on a mainstream media platform if they actually meant what they said! What they've successfully achieved is to establish a rare format in today's podcast landscape that's tapped into a growing audience who feel starved of the straight-talking culture Britain once had.

The 30mins of weekly banter is side-splitting, leaving me chuckling away whilst listening on an evening dog walk. However ridiculous it sounds, this weekly check in with sanity leaves me with temporary feeling of normality once again. In a small way it's proved to be a mini gamechanger for me over the last 3 years.

If you're brave enough, give it a go, but don't say that I didn't warn you!

Practitioners

I've encountered numerous members of the medical profession over recent years, the vast majority carrying a genuine desire to help. Having felt at times like I was nothing more than a widget moving through the factory line that is the UK public health system, I simply can't find the right words to articulate just how incredibly grateful I am that I had access to private treatment... something I WILL NEVER take for granted.

I've been fortunate enough to meet a small handful of remarkable practitioners I absolutely must acknowledge. I'll start with Siobhan Shalaby (Consultant Dietician). I've not seen Siobhan for a few years now but hold nothing but fond memories from the two years I spent in her care during my early days battling against anorexia. She wasn't able to fix me, mainly because I didn't actually want to be fixed at the time, but she sowed some early seeds that helped me take some initial steps out of the darkest phase of my illness. A tough talking

Irish lady who'd rightfully challenge my thinking in a robust way, but someone with a true heart of gold!

The second of my three is Bernie Wright, a councilor based in Tunbridge Wells (Kent) who specialises in the complex field of eating disorders. Bernie remains one of the most caring professionals I've ever had the fortune to encounter, carrying a soft tone, but most importantly she's someone who displayed a genuine understanding of the complexity I was dealing with. She also welcomed Kerry into her home on a number of occasions, supporting both of us during a time when the illness had spread deep into the heart of our marriage.

Finally, I have to say a huge thankyou to the lady who has proved instrumental in helping me over the last two years of my journey towards contentment. Joey Lessom is a Psychotherapist based in Forest Row (East Sussex), whom I still see periodically (to help keep me in check!). Another tough talking lady (noted, a is theme emerging) in her late 70's, still going strong in her professional life, running a clinic from both home and in London. Siobhan and Bernie both played a big part in my journey, but Joey has undoubtably been the person who unlocked the ability to finally take strides forward. Possibly an element of 'right place, right time' in terms of the maturity of my relationship with addiction when I first met Joey, but she's been the one who finally hammered home the messages I needed to hear and take note of.

CHAPTER 23
RIP Sid

During what's been first journey into writing Sidney Cockle passed away, aged 81. Born in 1941, Sidney, better known to all as 'Rob', entered this world in circumstances that a child should ever have to endure. We take early childhood memories of motherly affection for granted, but Rob never had the chance to meet the lady who brought him into this world. His mother tragically died during childbirth that left him in the care of secondary relatives who raised him as one of their own. His father was wholly absent from his life for reasons best left in the past.

A father of four, Tony, Mandy, Jenny and Suzanne, and grandfather to many (Cockle or not), Rob was a true family man who'd defend those close to him the type of loyalty you can't buy these days. I suspect this was his way of trying to correct the mistakes his own father made. He was a great all-round person, a humoured and loving character, yet carrying a notably short and protective fuse. He was a traditionalist at heart carrying an ethos of "mess with my family, you mess with me". With three daughters I've no doubt that boyfriends in the earlier days will have always treated them with the upmost of respect, even after they left emigrated to Australia in their teens... one slip and he'd have been on the next flight out of Heathrow!

Despite the circumstances in which Rob entered this world, he grew up to become a wonderful man, someone who brought love and laughter to family and friends throughout his life. Despite leaving school early with no qualifications, he was a smart cookie and rarely fooled. He entered working life as a "chippy" (carpenter) but got bored of life indoors which saw him turn to local council binman duty, 'working the dust' until the day he retired. Knowing him well he will have displayed the stereotypical traits of someone of his generation in the job …hard working and enjoying the banter with his workmates and the residents he served.

Renowned for his inability to sit still for more than 5 minutes, Rob always had a building project on the go. All the way up to the final months of his life, he'd never allowed himself to pay a tradesman, best illustrated by his superhero effort at the ripe old age of 80 to dig up and relay the concrete driveway leading to his house.

Rob was my step-grandfather. His son Tony, my stepdad, entered my life when I was 11, him being at the grand old age of 27 (at the time an old man in my eyes). I'm now 45 and look back at when Tony first took me under his wing. When I was 27, I don't think I could have taken on responsibility for someone else's child approaching their teens. Despite the absence of a blood relationship both Tony and Rob treated me as if I was a born and bred 'Cockle'.

During the school summer holidays I'd often go and stay with Rob, who by then had moved away from his longstanding home in Edgeware (London) to the small town of Walcott on the Norfolk coast. I've got fond memories of those times. He'd take me fishing, happy to sit by the lake all day despite having absolutely no interest or any of the essential patience needed. Renown for being a peaceful pastime, used by anglers to connect with nature, Rob didn't do low volume conversation, leaving the other anglers, even those on the opposite bank having to endure a day listening to his loud north London twang. I'll never forget the day he took me to see the comedian Freddie Star, at the theatre on Great Yarmouth pier …a brilliant evening that started with an early dinner in a pie and mash shop, proper binman style, followed by the entertainment watching Rob crying with his sides literally splitting with laughter.

Rob never addressed me by my actual name (Colin), always referring to me as "Col". I've always said to my mum that I will never forgive her my for the name she assigned me at birth, well known for its association with stupidity and odd-ball characters on TV sitcoms. I've always hated being referred to as 'Col'. But with Rob, and him alone, it didn't bother me one single bit. I never actually heard "Col", instead attaching myself to the affection in its delivery. At every opportunity when I was a teenager, he'd asked me… "you had your end away yet Col?". Whilst far from the type of language you'd expect from an elder in today's politically correct world, his banter was endless, usually followed by him cracking up over his own wise crack. I've got nothing but fond memories of my time spent with him as kid.

During the week before Rob passed, I did my best to support Tony following his dad's admission to hospital. Tony and Rob had a unique relationship, one you rarely see. They were genuine best mates, inseparable in many respects, and followed a strict weekly routine of contact. In my younger days, Rob would drive over to our house every Wednesday afternoon which coincided with Tony's half day at work. They'd talk for ages, usually about utter nonsense, simply because they enjoyed each other's company. I look back on this now and reflect on the relationship I had with my dad, envious of the strength of the bond between them.

Having gone through the whole experience with my father's passing I thought I'd be pretty hardened when it comes to dealing with death, but fond memories of Rob from days gone by has made it harder than I'd expected.

THE END

Printed in Great Britain
by Amazon